JEWELS WITHIN THE HEART

JEWELS WITHIN THE HEART

VERSES OF THE BUDDHA'S TEACHINGS
(DHAMMAPADA)

BY

LAURENCE-KHANTIPALO MILLS

SILKWORM BOOKS

May
I
dedicate the
merits of working
on this book to
all my Teachers in the various
manifestations of the Buddhasasana,
and to all my fellow-practitioners both
known and unknown. Without limitations
may they discover the Dharma's
Truth in their hearts, and all beings, those on the
path and those not yet upon it, rejoice in peace and

happiness.

ISBN 974-7100-73-8

This edition first published in 1999 by
Silkworm Books
Suriwong Book Centre Building, 54/1 Sridonchai Road,
Chiang Mai 50100, Thailand.
E-mail: silkworm@pobox.com

Cover design by T. Jittidejarak
Cover photograph © Copyright 1987 by Pundit Watanakasiwit
Set in 10.5 pt. Palatino

Printed by O.S. Printing House, Bangkok.

CONTENTS

PREFACE TO THE THIRD EDITION

This translation of the Dhammapada (Dhp.) verses is the third revision of work which appeared originally under the title *Growing the Bodhi Tree* published by The Buddhist Association of Thailand in 1966. In that version I had rearranged the order of the verses to suggest how one could grow the Bodhi Tree in the garden of the heart. That version, my first attempt at a verse translation and not a very good one, has long been out of print.

In *The Dhammapada – Path of Truth*, (Mahamakut Rajavidyalaya Press, Bangkok, 2520/1977), I reworked the translation and restored the traditional order of the verses. Two essays preceded the translation in the first of which I illustrated the Buddha's teaching by quoting a number Dhp. verses. The second essay, entitled 'Everyday Buddhism' also quoted Dhp. verses highlighting such matters as Enmity, Pride, Reliability, Friends and many more all within the framework of Dhp. 183:

> Every evil never doing
> and in wholesomeness increasing
> and one's heart well-purifying:
> this is the Buddhas' Teaching.

Then in 1990 Fo Kuang Publishing House in Taiwan

brought out a later revision of Dhp. This version contained a new introduction and an extensive reworking of the translation, together with the Pali verses.

Finally in the present book I have again simplified the verse translation and used mainly non-sexist language. Sometimes I have preferred to use earlier translations but occasional verses and many lines have been newly rendered. Another change is that I have preferred to use Sanskrit form of words left untranslated. Dharma and Nirvana for instance are better known than their Pali equivalents.

I hope that all readers will enjoy this brief collection of verses from the Buddhas' teaching – all the Buddhas teach an ancient Dharma or Law which is true whatever the world's changes – as much as I have had joy in translating them. This work would not have reached completion without the typing done by my wife and kalyānamitri, Dammika.

My thanks also to Trasvin Jittidejarak of Silkworm Books for encouraging me to revise my Dhammapada translation for publication.

May all sentient beings reach the
Place of Peace.

Laurence C R Mills
(formerly Phra Khantipalo)
Bodhi Citta Buddhist Centre
P O Box 8177
Cairns QLD 4870
10 November 1996   Australia

INTRODUCTION TO THE BUDDHA'S TEACHING

The path of Buddhist practice is the way of training the mind together with the good which is produced by doing this, for other sentient beings in the world. The mind, the heart, (unfortunately English does not have a word combining intellect and emotions) which is not trained is 'wild' creating suffering both for oneself and others.

Dharma, the natural law, the peaceful way, the path of training taught by the Buddha Sakyamuni, cannot rightly be practised selfishly, since its direction is towards the diminishment and finally disappearance through insight, of the trouble-causing idea of self. When properly practised, Dharma always benefits not only the doer but other beings human and otherwise, near and far away. When one person begins to practise Dharma it is like taking up one knot in a net, an action which causes many and eventually all, of that net's knots to move. In the same way the practice even when it is just beginning has an incalculable effect.

The Buddha, in teaching about four kinds of people, praised one particular. There were, he said, those persons who benefit only themselves, those who benefit others, those benefiting both themselves and others and those who benefit neither. The last category obviously includes all those who live thoroughly selfish and possibly destructive lives, while the first though concerned with some sort of benefit are limited to themselves. The second class is too one-sided as their concern to benefit others leads them to neglect themselves. The Buddha praised those who benefit both themselves and others as "best and highest, foremost, greatest and supreme". He was indeed the greatest example of this very teaching.

This brief introduction will outline the Buddha's teachings using as a framework the traditional division of Dharma into virtue, meditation and wisdom as illustrated by the famous Dhammapada (Dhp.) verse called the Heart of the Buddha's Instructions:

> Every evil never doing
> And in wholesomeness increasing
> And one's heart well purifying
> This is the Buddhas' Teaching. (Dhp. 183)

The first line will serve as a heading for the section on virtue, the second for meditation and other good actions, while the third will head an explanation of wisdom. Under the fourth line the universality of the Buddhas' Dharma will be considered.

A final section will give some information on the Dhammapada as a Buddhist Scripture and the place it has held in the hearts and practice of Buddhists through the ages.

EVERY EVIL NEVER DOING

Evil is what harms oneself and sometimes others too. It consists of deliberate actions (karma) of speech and body which are motivated by greed, hatred or delusion, the prime sources of human suffering. Such actions should not be done as they will result in either immediate or delayed pain for the doer. This is an illustration of karma and its results: these are the quite natural results of destructive or harmful actions. Therefore, as we are all beings who do not like to suffer but wish for happiness, we have to learn not to create for ourselves and others the conditions producing suffering. If someone went around with a viper as a pet feeding and fondling it under the impression that this would lead to happiness, people would say he was mad. At least let the viper go, that will be a beginning on the path to peace! Likewise, while we do only, or mostly, those actions productive of suffering, 'nursing our vipers', we cannot expect to find real happiness, peace or contentment.

This is the general reason for leading a virtuous life but there are more detailed reasons as well involving the benefit of oneself and others, which have already been mentioned. The person who benefits and does not harm his/herself must be truly wise, for only a fool would do otherwise. Also, this person who acts for their own benefit will properly consider others' benefit as well: this is a compassionate person, one who does not wish to increase the sufferings in the world but to grow others in happiness and peace. Therefore the true practice of virtue involves harming neither oneself nor others but the benefit of both, this being the way of growing in wisdom and compassion. These two virtues, at first seemingly separate but finally known as the same, run all the way through the practice of Dharma.

If a person has no virtue they cannot proceed to the higher practice, such as meditation. Trying to do otherwise would be like attempting to erect walls on a building that lacked a foundation. That moral foundation is provided in Dharma by the essence of virtue called the Five Precepts. (Virtue, morality, precepts are all the same word – sīla, in Pali.) These Five Precepts, to be considered below, were selected by the Buddha to restrain the most harmful human activities, beginning of course with killing.

1. "I undertake the training-rule to refrain from killing living beings".

When a person undertakes this training they will be as gentle as possible and try not to kill deliberately any creature, large or small. If one kills unintentionally, as when one steps on a tiny ant that cannot be seen, or when travelling and insects die by impact on the windscreen, this precept is not broken. The intention to kill has to be present for that to occur. It may not always be possible, at home or at work, to avoid killing sentient beings, as when one has to defend one's house against termites, but even then mercy should prevail and the least harmful but effective measures should be taken. Of course, this precept primarily concerns the taking of human life, a possibility which does not arise for most people. In this case, it is possible to justify killing in self-defence where no other means, less drastic, will preserve one's life. It may also be possible to justify taking part in a defensive war, though preferably as a non-combatant such as a member of the medical corps, when one's country is in danger. Apart from such exceptions as these, other intentional killings must count as murder, crimes which all countries agree to be the most serious. Even then of course, there are differences as between a murder long-planned and contemplated and one done in the heat of anger. Worse results attend the first, from a karmic point of view, than the second where the results will be slighter. It is interesting to note that the laws of various countries agree with this and inflict different penalties for the first and second degree murder. Motivation for killing is usually hatred but may in some circumstances be greed (as in hunting) or delusion (as when animals are sacrificed, supposedly to gain the good will of the gods). Another fact to be examined here is the purity and intelligence of the being killed. The swatting of a mosquito is obviously not as serious as the intentional killing of a dog. Much more effort must be put into the latter than the former, more effort and stronger intention. When we compare the killing of a dog with the murder of a human being we find, as the law agrees, that the latter is much more serious. Karmically, the fruit or result from the latter action will be much heavier. In fact, the heaviness of the result increases with the purity of the individual killed, with the murder of an enlightened person the most disastrous of all. In Buddhist teachings, the killing of one's parents is also regarded as a sure cause for bad rebirth in the next life. The noble qualities which are developed through keeping this precept are loving-kindness, the sort of love which can be extended to all beings, and compassion, concern with the sufferings of others leading one to help them in appropriate ways.

2. "I undertake the training-rule to refrain from taking what is not given".

This rule encompasses, by the phrase 'taking what is not given', all sorts of actions which people do not call stealing but which in fact are a kind of theft. Such words as ' scrumping' (for apples hanging on another's tree), ' borrowing' (a book which one has no intention of returning), 'making use of' (`surplus' government or business supplies for oneself), express such types of theft. Outright theft, whether it is 'ripping off' a supermarket, burglary or fiddling the company's books, are all included here. All sorts of fraudulent business deals including illegal jugglery with stocks and shares, must find a place also under this precept. So will computer crimes, whether involving the theft of money or of data. And then there are ways of 'taking what is not given' as when an employer ' takes' the work of employees but badly underpays them, or when workers take their pay packets, cheques etc. but have not done the work they were supposed to do. The heaviness of the result will obviously vary with the type of karma made, with factors like the extent of the planning required, the harm done and the material stolen, to be taken into consideration. One can even steal by not taking anything away, as when boundary marks are moved in one's own favour while theft is also committed by the non-payment of dues charged on certain articles by the government, as in smuggling. The motivation for all this is obviously greed: more and more for me (and my family). The strength of the greed involved will determine the karmic result. Obviously the quality of the persons from whom one steals will also affect the karmic result, which may be clearly understood by taking the extreme cases of stealing from another thief as contrasted with theft from a pure-living community of monks and nuns. It is said, though this must be rare enough, that stealing the meagre possessions of a monk or nun who is enlightened will entail the heaviest results of all. The quality reckoned as noble that is developed through practising this precept is that one's livelihood is a pure one (involving no harm to living beings) and inspires others too to lead a good life.

3. "I undertake the training-rule to refrain from wrong conduct in sexual relations".

This is sometimes seen translated as refraining "from adultery" but this is only one kind of wrong conduct in sexual relations. Certainly a person keeping this precept will be careful not to cause sufferings of grief and remorse by having sex with one partner of an established relationship. They must also ensure that their sexual pleasures involves no harm to themselves or to others. Some obvious examples of actions or persons to be avoided are, rape, molesting children and all sado-masochistic practices. If the yardstick of 'neither harming oneself nor others' is kept in mind it should be fairly easy to determine what should and should not be done but in this, the present precept is no different from the others. The Buddhist ethic in all the precepts is to live with an understanding self-restraint. In the case of this precept this should banish both negligent indulgence on one side and repressiveness and guilt on the other. Motivation in breaking this precept is usually greed under the name of lust, a very powerful driving force as everyone knows. Results will be worse when instead of being driven by indulgent lust, actions are motivated by hatred. The gravity of bad karma made under this precept naturally varies with strength of intention, repeated actions and the type of persons involved. Traditional sources state that if an enlightened nun or monk is raped that would be the worst possible bad karma here. Contentment is the noble quality developed through practising this precept, leading first to much happiness in life whether one is married or single and then to a peaceful mind.

4. "I undertake the training-rule to refrain from false speech".

False speech or lying is what departs from the truth and at least will harm the utterer and possibly others too. It is usually motivated by delusion variously coloured by greed and hatred so that it can in no way be praised as a good action. Experience may require, on occasions, the utterance of lies as when more sufferings will result should the whole truth be told but this should not become a habit! The habit of lying is like patching an old cloth – the patches are the lies required to cover up the holes. More holes require more patches. One ends up with a cloth of more patches than anything else and finally reaches the state where no one will believe a word one says! As Buddhists are aiming through practice to discover the truth in their own hearts, if they lie or commit the other forms of false speech, they will lead themselves in the opposite direction. Under the heading of Wrong Speech are also slander, harsh speech and gossip. Their opposites known as the fourfold Right Speech are truth-speaking, speech leading to concord between people, friendly words and meaningful talk worth remembering. These are good qualities developed by guarding one's mouth, leading one to live in a harmonious environment and further to the happiness of others who will come to trust in one's words. The result of breaking this precept will vary with the reason why the falsehood was uttered, the degree of selfishness involved in its utterance, the other people who are affected for the worse by it and the person to whom the lie was addressed. It is said that lying to an eminent teacher of Dharma is very bad, while a lie spoken to an enlightened person is worst of all. Of course, being enlightened they may see right through one's feeble fabric of lies!

5. "I undertake the training-rule to refrain from all intoxicants confusing the mind".

The Pali text here has literally "from distillations (brandy, whisky, rum, gin, etc), fermentations (beer, wine, cider) and intoxicators (really 'maddeners' meaning all kinds of drugs injected, inhaled, etc.) which are an occasion for carelessness". This leaves very few loopholes! As the purpose of this Dharma is to train the mind in clarity, it makes no sense to confuse it more than it is already. The motivation for doing so is of course just delusion: the mistaken belief that drink or drugs will help one to deal with the great sufferings one experiences. All they do is to dull the mind and make it less perceptive so that the sufferings appear to go away, only to return with much more force later. In the long run they destroy all the brightness of the mind leading to a complete dominance of delusion as with drug addicts, alcoholics and those who are senile. While 'under the influence' all sorts of things can be done of which one would not normally approve, these intoxicants thus becoming real 'occasions for care-lessness' when all the precepts can be broken. There are occasions when one must use one's wisdom in practising this precept, as when, for instance, refusing a single drink will offend one's hosts. The principle to remember is never to become drunk nor to become addicted – and nor, of course, to delude oneself or let others delude one, that one is not already 'hooked' and that another glass, smoke or whatever it is, will be quite alright. The karmic results of breaking this precept will also vary, according to frequency and the substances used, (there are obvious differences between downing an occasional beer and drinking a bottle of whisky a day!) Generally, the result is bound to be a clouding of the mind in this life and rebirth as a stupid person, (if one makes it to a human existence), next time. As to the noble quality developed with this precept, that is the most valuable of all: mindfulness and clear awareness. More will be said about these in the next section. The worst possible karma to make would be to deliberately cause another person to become addicted and so destroy their mind.

There are numerous advantages of keeping these precepts, many of which will have become clear in the last few pages. Here a few more points may be added in their favour. As far as personal happiness is concerned, these precepts lead to good fortune, what is truly lucky or auspicious. In the Buddha's days, as in our own, people tended to be superstitious and regarded various omens as lucky or unlucky, not knowing that the real 'luck' is living an honest and compassionate life, while the greatest misfortune or bad luck comes about by making bad karma in breaking these precepts. So, if good fortune is your aim in life these precepts are a sure guide to it.

Another personal benefit which often results from keeping the precepts is longevity. When the precepts are kept reasonably well, (everyone breaks a precept occasionally!) then lack of worry and no remorse is the result. With a few worries why should one not live long? After having enjoyed a long life and dying peacefully with no regrets the next benefit will be an excellent human rebirth. There is no need to worry about animal birth or other painful destinies when the Five Precepts have been consistently kept well. They are referred to as the Human Dharma and guarantee a truly human mind which will lead to a birth amongst humans with good opportunities of every sort.

Family benefits should be mentioned too. In a family where most people keep the precepts quarrels will be avoided and it will be possible to live in a peaceful house. This is a great blessing as family life is the fundamental unit of society producing future generations who should be able to learn peaceful and virtuous ways from their parents.

On the social level, the benefit of many people keeping the precepts is obviously going to be less crime and more harmony. Most of us would like to live in a society where crime was not a problem and where people lived together more harmoniously. This need not be an impractical ideal! All that is necessary for this to happen is for large numbers of people really to try to keep the precepts. The marvellous result of this is that police forces, prisons and most of the legal profession will be needed no more, while armies and other armed forces can be disbanded and the resources they now consume turned to more peaceful ends.

All these are wonderful results of keeping precepts! Inspire yourself to make a better world possible for all the living beings in it!

There are various traditional ways of regarding the

precepts according to the lineage of Buddhist teachers from whom one has received them. Here three of them will be mentioned. In the Theravada countries of South and South-East Asia, all five precepts are undertaken frequently. Buddhist ceremonies at temples and in houses often begin with lay people undertaking the Three Refuges (to be outlined at the end) and the Five Precepts from a senior monk. It is assumed that people will break the precepts and so need to renew their commitment to them. To do so privately or with one's family every day in one's shrine room is a good thing but of course if they are mindlessly repeated with many other people as just part of a ritual they lose all their significance.

By contrast, in Chinese, Korean and Vietnamese traditions, precepts are taken once and then only when one is sure of being able to keep them. People in this tradition may Go for Refuge (and thus proclaim themselves Buddhists) while not undertaking the precepts as they fear they will not be able to keep them. This is a way of regarding the precepts as a serious commitment and certainly avoids the disadvantage mentioned above of ritualising them. It may lead to smaller numbers of people undertaking the precepts but they will be more committed to their practice.

Another way of regarding the precepts is only to undertake those which one can keep. In Tibetan tradition, it is possible to be a one-precepter, two-precepter and so on. This is a rather practical arrangement and avoids the kind of situation where people undertake to keep all five precepts but know that they will break one or more of them frequently. After practising one or two precepts initially, a person's life may change so that they wish to practice all of them. This method also shows genuine commitment to practice.

The Dhammapada contains many verses on making evil karma, see for instance 66-69 and 71, 117 and 119, 121, 125, 127, 161, 162. Though the precepts are not mentioned as such, two verses, 246-7, list the five things not to be done, while the breaking of the third precept is the subject of verses 309-10. The results of evil karma directed against good people (particularly those who are enlightened) is vividly related at 137-140. The making of good karma, not specially with reference to the precepts though, is often found in paired verses, the first about evil, the second on goodness. Such verses may be found as in: 16, 18, 68, 116, 118, 122, 132 and so on.

AND IN WHOLESOMENESS INCREASING

'Wholesomeness' means healthy states of mind that tend to be whole or concentrated and ultimately holy. (It is interesting to note that whole, hale, healthy and holy are all related words). Wholesome mind-states are those where generosity / renunciation, loving-kindness / compassion and wisdom / understanding are strong. Good karma is made with such factors of Dharma, mind-karma, which may then be translated into speech and body karmas. Society can only run smoothly when large numbers of people make such karma, so that people can trust each other. On the other hand, fear and anxiety increase in individuals and therefore in society, when such good karmas are not made and when trust in others cannot be established. Wholesomeness is best increased not by wanting to make good karma but by getting down to doing it. What does one do?

1. Generosity

No kind of spiritual life can grow without real heartfelt generosity. 'Heartfelt' means that one gives in a non-calculating way, without desire for gifts in return or fame and with 'unsticky hands' as Buddhist works describe it. One does not regret giving, nor try to control what was given. What can be given? Obviously, wealth, help, skills, time – there is no limit to the subject of giving. It joins forces with giving up or renunciation and that in turn leads to unselfish, non-egoistic practice of meditation and ultimately to the letting-go of self. Giving is a large subject! Buddhist tradition has often divided it into the gift of non-fear which is another way of speaking of loving-kindness (see below), the gift of material things for which Buddhist people in every country are famous (see any Buddhist temple festival, or celebration at home), and the gift of Dharma (learned Buddhists give in this way by lecturing and advising people, as well as by writing and making the Dharma available through the media).

2. Loving-kindness and Compassion

These qualities increase in anyone who is generous. They are produced by the good practice of the rest of the Dharma but may be stimulated by some reflections and meditations. Here is a brief one suitable for learning by heart and chanting to oneself in all sorts of situations:

"May I be happy;

may I be free from suffering;
may I be free from enmity;
may I be free from hurtfulness;
may I be free from troubles of mind and body;
may I be able to protect my own happiness".

"Whatever beings there are -
may they be happy;
may they be free from suffering;
may they be free from enmity;
may they be free from hurtfulness;
may they be free from troubles of mind and body;
may they be able to protect their own happiness".

These kinds of reflections will lead to more loving-kindness or gentleness with oneself (and so, less hatred) and better relations with other people and 'difficult' animals such as spiders and snakes. Eventually one's heart begins to open up so that one can feel some love there and this in turn can lead to extended mind-states centred on a love which is infinite and expressed in the same way to all beings. Thoughts of compassion can be stimulated by contemplating the amount and variety of sufferings found in this world – 'the ocean of sufferings' as Buddhists call them. As one's mind becomes more sensitive to them one will become increasingly careful not to cause more suffering and where it is possible, to lessen the sufferings of others. This subject naturally leads on to the next.

3. Helpfulness and Service

This is an excellent way of overcoming selfish desires while lessening others' sorrows. It is also related to the next subject as when one serves one's Dharma teacher. The occasions and ways of practising helpfulness are legion and so cannot be listed. All that is necessary is to keep one's eyes open and mind alert!

4. Respectfulness

A number of related actions are included here such as being respectful to parents and to teachers at school (if this is absent one cannot express gratitude to the first nor learn from the second); reverence expressed towards Dharma teachers by such actions as bowing down, 'lotusing' one's hands and addressing them properly; the same actions performed before a shrine where there is a Buddha-image, or outside round a pagoda; the circumambulation of either of the last two symbols of Enlightenment; and last, the asking for forgiveness from parents, teachers or friends, and the granting of forgiveness (by not hanging on to resentment) to other people, either in one's heart or in words spoken at the right time.

5. Meditation

A vast subject that can only be outlined here. The ordinary states of mind are 'wild', they come and go as they will without regard to what produces happiness and suffering or what will lead to these experiences in others. Wild minds are unhappy minds and spread unhappiness around them. Generally speaking they consist of thoughts of sense-pleasures and of ill-will, together with attacks of lethargy and drowsiness, agitation and worry and some-times sceptical doubt. These are called the five hindrances by the Buddha but we look upon them as normal mental states. They all produce sufferings. They all arise conditionally. They may all be eradicated when the conditions producing them have vanished.

Then what kind of mind will one have? It will be a bright mind not grasping after sensual desires nor tormented by ill-will; it will not be slothful and drowsy, or agitated by unending thoughts, worries or remorse; it will be a mind free from uncertainty because it has experienced the growth of good states. Would it not be nice to have a mind like this? Meditation, when Buddhists use the word, means emptying our the mind, not filling it up with pious thoughts. As the mind is naturally pure there is no need to strive after artificially 'religious' states. Just let it be. But this is hard at first because mind is used to grasping after ideas and memories, plans and hopes, fears and fantasies. These are the causes of suffering. These are the five hindrances. Let these hindrances which produce unending turmoil in the world die down.

How is that to be done? The breath goes in and out of the body constantly. Watch it! Let the mind be aware of it. Constantly bring the mind back to the breath. Breath is peaceful and it always occurs now. Let the mind know this peaceful now. Be patient and take this mind-medicine regularly.

Sit regularly every day preferably at the same time and to begin with, for not less than half an hour. Sit up straight and do not let the body slump or the head nod. If possible sit in lotus or half-lotus positions as these are good for the growth of awareness. If not possible, sit on a firm chair but do not lean against the back. Once seated comfortably in meditation posture do not move the body even slightly. Endure pain by being mindful of it (see below). Do not expect to get anything from your meditation. Not calm, not peace, not happiness – just sit. These things will happen by themselves and must not be sought after. Neither should one get attached to any 'experience' that may occur. If they do, just let them arise and pass away. If pleasant, do not want them to recur. If unpleasant, do not reject them. Good 'sits' may be followed by what are, according to one's judgement, 'bad' sits. Do not want the one nor reject the other. Just sit and attend closely. Eventually mind-states may arise which are peaceful, pure and very extensive. That is the good result of regular mind-work. Do not become attached to them but use them to deepen concentration. If not before, by this time you will need advice from a well-qualified meditation teacher whose pupil you will become. These vast areas of the mind, ('my' mind which 'I' thought 'I' knew so well), are rather like the unexplored areas of the world on western maps a century or two ago.

Out of these deep concentrations of mind various strange things may begin to happen. This is the beginning of the development of psychical powers which are very dangerous to people who are not training themselves according to Dharma. Do not become interested in these things which will prove only a sidetrack off the main path of Dharma. Experienced teachers can use these powers for much benefit of others who train with them but trainees should not be fascinated by them.

In this brief account only one meditation subject, mindfulness of breathing, has been mentioned though there are many other ways taught in the various schools of Buddhism. Breath-meditation is widely known and used both in Theravada and in Ch'an/Zen, while it is also employed in more complex ways in Tibetan meditations.

6. Mindfulness

One cannot always be sitting in meditation but the meditative mind can be extended to other situations with mindfulness. This is a general term which includes awareness of the body's actions (as in breathing), movements and postures, its contents and its eventual decay; awareness of feelings, pleasant, painful and neutral; awareness of 'minds' (one's own varying mind-stream); and awareness of the content of mind with a view to noticing their arising and passing away, an aspect of insight-wisdom to be explained under the next heading.

Different aspects of mindfulness are suitable for various sorts of characters. For instance, distracted people are usually recommended to practise mindfulness of breathing, while lustful characters should inspect the contents of the body beginning with "hair of the head, hair of the body, nails, teeth and skin". Emotional people will find mindfulness of feeling suitable but those who have already some calm will profit from mindfulness of the mind, which is actually mind watching the mind. Very sharp and perceptive persons may employ mindfulness of mental contents with great advantage. A meditation master should be consulted as to what kind of practice will be suited to one's character.

With mindfulness which can be practised in every action, gradually the whole of one's life becomes Dharma practice and every situation is a chance to penetrate the Dharma for oneself. These two aspects of meditation, calm and mindfulness, complement each other and while people may incline more to one than the other, all need to balance these two aspects.

The development of mindfulness in which one notes the impermanence, the arising and passing, of all perceptions, sensations, thoughts and consciousness leads on to the next topic.

AND ONE'S HEART WELL-PURIFYING

Wisdom finds out the truth of these teachings for oneself. What does this wisdom know? It knows the real nature of conditioned phenomena – our world of eye and sights, ear and sounds, nose and smells, tongue and tastes, body and touches, mind and thoughts. All these arise conditionally, exist due to conditions and pass away when those conditions cease. We 'know' it (marginally, sometimes), but for liberation we must know it as it really is all the time. The Diamond Sutra, a famous Buddhist Scripture, has this verse;

> "As stars, a fault of vision or a lamp,
> deceptive trick, a rain-cloud or a bubble,
> a dream, a lightning-flash, a drop of dew:
> so should be viewed all that is conditioned".

All these metaphors for our everyday experience point in a way opposite to the one we are accustomed. When I see a flower the notion of myself as a stable entity arises, 'peering out' as it were from 'my' eyeballs at the flower, another fairly stable thing, which if attractive, 'I' want. What a mess! No such stable entities exist as my self, no owner who is me, no parts like eyeballs that could be owned and no stable objects as flowers, people, possessions which could be unchangingly grasped. We are invited by the Buddha to regard all this conditioned, highly unstable existence as 'stars', remote, feebly-winking lights in the immense impersonal blackness of space! If we have not practised meditation to make our minds firm and secure, we must surely be scared stiff of regarding our everyday experience in this way! The other metaphors, showing the faultiness of our ordinary perception (dots in the eyes), conditionedness (a lamp), the attached mind's tricky con-jurations (a deceptive trick), the false appearance of solidity (rain-cloud), evanescence (bubble), insubstantiality and inability to master (a dream), the momentary nature of immense power (a lightning-flash), fragility and utter fleet-ingness especially of beauty (a drop of dew), all present us with ways of opening the mind and letting go of notions of being and substance.

So, the 'conditioned' that is the whole of our life, inside and outside, mental-emotional and physical, is all im-permanent and cannot be grasped successfully. No security will be gained by doing so for most 'secure' worldly things can be, at most, enjoyed until death. Many such 'securities', money, jewellery, property, buildings, businesses, clothes, investments and so on, prove their unstable condition by vanishing against our wishes even before that time. This is why the Buddha taught that wealth given away to noble causes was a true possession (as the good karma stored in one's heart), while hoarded wealth was really lost and wasted.

Clinging to impermanent, changeful experience, even this body, even this mind, its memories, its hopes and fears, can never produce real security. All it produces is the suffering of fear and anxiety. To a body that must at least suffer the pains of birth, decay, disease and death we add, as though we had not enough sufferings yet, the mental-

xxix

emotional torture of trying to pretend some permanent person called: 'I, me, myself', exists surrounded by my permanent assets, all of them 'mine'. How crazy can we get?

Then the question arises, 'Who knows all that is conditioned?' It seems beyond the ordinary attached mind to understand that the conditioned can continue quite well without 'I, me, myself'. Even this body, which by some enormous conceit I call 'mine', the heart goes on pumping, the kidneys go on straining, the guts go on digesting, quite without any control exercised by 'me'. And if we are meditators, we shall know that thoughts arise and pass away quite without any authority of 'mine', yet with some degree of madness 'I' call it 'my mind'.

Voidness is the experience of conditionedness without any one experiencing it. 'I' am absent when it happens. And this is a liberating experience in which all the greed, hatred and delusion, all the five hindrances, all the duality of subject-object, vanishes and there is just that. Sometimes called Thusness, the way it really is, the Unconditioned, Nirvana or Enlightenment, it is not somewhere else, sometime else, it has always been here and now. It is our everyday life seen newly, without distortion.

From the point of view of unenlightened persons like ourselves, we ordinary people are far away from Buddhas and Arahants. But those who have known and seen, do not perceive it thus. For them, ordinary folks and Buddhas are all the same.

Unenlightened people think that defilements and the enlightened mind are far different. But Buddhas know that enlightened mind and defilements are all void in their nature.

Ordinary people have heard that they are on the fearful hither shore, a metaphor for the round of birth and death, saṁsāra, while the Buddhas stand secure on the further shore of nirvāna. The former must make efforts to cross over the great river of craving to attain the incomparable security from bondage. But then so many great enlightened teachers have told us that saṁsāra and nirvāna are not different and that if only we would open our eyes we would find that we are already there – with nowhere to go.

THIS IS THE BUDDHAS' TEACHING

Many Buddhas, not only the historical figure of Sakya-muni, have according to him, taught this Dharma. All Buddhas, as they wake up to the same Dharma, the same truth, teach in the same way.

This truthful Dharma is never out of date, for humanity's condition always presents the same problems, the same sufferings. Besides being "not a matter of time" it is also true everywhere in the universe, wherever there are sentient beings, whatever they look like.

The Buddha does not command us to believe this Dharma, he asks us to investigate it in ourselves. We may reject it if we wish to do so but truth goes on being truth whether it is accepted or not. We should, if we are wise, investigate this liberating Dharma which at all times and all places is "inviting us to come and see". We should approach this investigation in the spirit of an ancient Buddhist Sanskrit verse:

> As one who's wise with gold
> smelts, cuts, on touchstone rubs,

so monks, accept my words
with wisdom, not belief.

A good goldsmith does not assume the purity of a sample of gold, she/he tests it first. In the same way, the Buddha's words are not to be accepted by blind belief (literally, 'out of respect for the guru') but must be investigated with wisdom.

As we practise this Dharma we may wish to go for Refuge to the Buddha, the Awakened One, to the Dharma, the Path to Awakening and to the Sangha, the Community of those Awakened by practising that Path, and we may say with deep conviction of the rightness, truth and compassionate nature of our practice:

"To the Buddha I go for refuge
To the Dharma I go for refuge
To the Sangha I go for refuge".

These are safe refuges as the Buddha explains in verses 188-192 in the translation.

We may or we may not wish to emphasise our commitment to practice, to deepen our practice of the Way by following in the footsteps of the Buddha and trying to generate his compassionate heart through the recitation of the four Great Vows:

Though sentient beings are numberless,
I vow to lead them crossing over.
Though greed, hatred and delusion rise endlessly,
I vow to exhaust them.
Though Dharma-gates are countless,
I vow to wake to them.

Though Buddha's Way is unsurpassed,
I vow to embody it fully.

To round off this introduction there is a well-known story about the Dhammapada verse we have used. In the days of the T'ang Dynasty a famous poet, Bai Ju-i who was also a minister at court, heard that a certain ascetic monk, known as the Bird's Nest Ch'an Master, who lived in the mountains had come to know the essence of Buddhism. As he had an intense desire to find that out for himself, he organised a journey to the foot of the mountain. After arriving there, he had to leave his palanquin and ascend the steep mountain on foot, arriving eventually at the secluded abode of the Ch'an Master. After he had paid his respects and recovered his breath he asked this question, ' What is the essence of Buddhism?' Perhaps he expected an esoteric secret in reply. What he received was a verse:

> "Every evil never doing
> And in wholesomeness increasing
> And one's heart well purifying;
> This is the Buddhas' teaching".

'But', he objected 'every child in the whole empire knows this verse!' 'Yes', replied the Ch'an Master, 'but old people with long white hair find it hard to practise'.

DHAMMAPADA AS A BUDDHIST SCRIPTURE

More than thirty translations of the Dhammapada (Dhp.) from Pali have now appeared in English. This makes it by far the best known Buddhist Scripture in 'western' countries. No doubt this is because it is not so long, consists of verses which can be easily read (if not so easily practised!) and appeals to peoples' imagination with the similes and metaphors frequently employed in its verse.

Here we shall glance briefly at the Dhp's history, as far as we know it and then consider some points about the present translation.

Though the Dhp's famous opening verses do look like a logical beginning, while the last chapter on the enlightened person's mind and actions is surely a fitting end, yet in between the arrangement of the material is best called poetic, or even perhaps to modern minds provided with so many systems for classification, chaotic. This points out Dhp's very ancient origins and to circumstances which we can now hardly imagine – an oral tradition passed down through generations of monks and nuns who learned the text by heart. Once a text has been learnt by heart it is difficult to insert anything into it or to rearrange it, at best more material may be added to the end, as had happened possibly in Dhp. with a large section of the last chapter which occurs elsewhere in the Pali Suttas.

Where did Dhp. originate? Individual verses, sometimes pairs and occasional larger groups, were no doubt spoken by the Buddha on many different occasions. We do not know who compiled this Dhp., no traditions have survived even in the Pali Commentaries to tell us about this. Perhaps it was the personal 'notebook' of verses that its collector liked, accumulated over years of listening to the Buddha's preaching. There is no doubt that the Buddha was an accomplished poet (he would have been trained in the art of spontaneous verse as part of his princely education) and that he recapitulated and emphasised his teachings given in prose with a verse or two at the end. The Dhp. verses are a collection of such verses without the contexts in which they were spoken.

About half of these verses are found elsewhere in the Pali Suttas. This raises a problem of where the other verses have come from. Presumably quite a lot of the Buddha's discourses have been lost and these verses, not found in the present Sutta collections, survive from that lost material.

As the Dhammapada qualified for preservation, not only being passed on orally but receiving the additional stamp of approval from the early Buddhist Councils, it must have had from the beginning high prestige. This fact points to a compiler who was a very eminent, possibly enlightened, monk or nun whose work in preserving these verses could not be neglected.

Why was this collection called Dhp.? Literally its meaning is Verses on the Law, Truth, or the Way which seems a straightforward title. However, the compound 'Dhammapada' is used elsewhere in the Suttas and there seems to mean a special kind of verse, possibly the verses, mentioned above, which recapitulate the teaching at the end of a prose discourse. One feature of these verses which is very well marked in Dhp. is either a single verse in which there are contrasting 'light' and 'dark' halves –

> From attachment grief is born,
> from attachment fear,
> one who is attachment-free
> has no grief – how fear? (Dhp. 215)

– or a pair of verses, one 'dark', one 'bright':

> If one should some evil do
> then do it not again, again.

Do not wish for it anew
for evil grows to pain.

If one should some merit make
do it then again, again.
One should wish for it anew
for merit grows to joy. (Dhp. 117–118)

These are perhaps some characteristics of Dhamma-padas – the Verses of Dharma.

Dhammapadas may be used in another plural sense if we consider the different Buddhist traditions which have survived down to our times and preserved a number of Dhp. recensions. At present we have besides the Pali Dhp. three (or four according to the Dict. of Chinese Buddhist Terms) translated at various times into Chinese. Two of them have been rather poorly translated into English, one by a Christian clergyman in the last century and one recently brought out in Belgium. One or possibly two Dhps have survived (partly) in Sanskrit and one of these is currently appearing in a Buddhist journal translated into English from French.

Another Dhp., the so-called Gandhari Dhp., has been partly recovered from the sands of central Asia but not so far been translated. Then there is a Tibetan Dhp. which has received two translations into English, one of them a modern and accurate rendering. Some of these Dhps are not known as such but called Udanavarga, The Inspired Chapters. This is the case with the Sanskrit, some of the Chinese translations and the Tibetan work. Most of these works are, or were longer than the 423 verses of the Pali Dhp. The material included in them however, is very much the same as the Pali verses though it is arranged in different ways and includes chapters which are absent from the Pali recension. No one particular version can claim to be the ' original' Dhp., rather all these versions must be traced back to a common source.

The Pali Dhp. in time collected material which solidified as a Commentary (Comy). This Comy, unchanged for 1500 years since the age of the commentator-monks, consists of two parts, one commenting on the meanings of words in the verses and the other telling a background story when a verse, or group of verses, was uttered by the Buddha. The former has only just been translated into English, a scholarly work recently published by Oxford University Press. The latter has long been available as "Buddhist Legends" published at first as three volumes in the Harvard Oriental Series. In recent years they have been reprinted by the Pali Text Society, Oxford, U.K.

In the notes following each chapter these stories have sometimes been referred to. Those who are interested should purchase the three volumes of this commentary and read them as there are many excellent tales, some of them very humorous. However, the connection between some verses and their stories appears quite unconvincing, while some of the less interesting stories obviously have been concocted to fit the verses. There are groups of verses which must have been spoken together (such as vv. 1–2) but which have separate stories, while there are also single stories in connection with which many verses were said to have been spoken, even though separate occasions seem more likely. Some stories are too exaggerated, specially in regard to magical powers, while in other places Dhp. verses which are in the male gender are reputed to be connected with incidents involving women. Though one may be doubtful about some of these stories being the occasion for Dhp. verses, yet there are many interesting, even inspiring, stories in this large collection.

Traditional Buddhist education of young monks and novices in Theravada countries has always involved some learning of the Dhammapada. In Sri Lanka, novices often learn the whole 423 verses by heart before they have studied Pali language which means that they know little or nothing of what they are memorising! Later on they will understand the verses and be able to use them together with the commentarial stories in sermons. In Thailand, the Comy is studied to pass one of the grades of Pali examinations. In this case the verses are learnt along with their Comy, a very traditional way of learning. All Theravada traditions use the Dhp. and Comy for teaching lay people. The latter often know far more about these stories than they do of the Suttas, in fact together with the Jatakas (stories of the Buddha's previous lives), this forms the source of most of their teachings.

The position of the various versions of Dhp. in northern Buddhist countries has not been so prominent largely due to the vast corpus of Mahāyāna works which have tended to obscure the earlier Buddhist Canon. In our days with the growth of a much larger educated laity, works like Dhp. are emerging from their neglect and again becoming prominent.

SURPRISING ASPECTS OF DHAMMAPADA

Generally, people assume that as the Pāli Dhp. is counted among Theravada Scriptures and included therefore in the Sutta-collections, its verses will always teach Dharma consistent with Theravada's more scholastic doctrines.

Such an assumption, however, proves false when a close examination is made of these verses as the following examples will show.

Dhp verses 1 and 2 open with an emphasis common to all Buddhist traditions – the primacy of mind. Mind as the Creator, mind as the origin of all dharmas (events), mind as the maker of all good and evil, receives more emphasis however, among the Mahāyāna philosophers of Yogācāra. That teaching really makes plain how all the experience of the world through the five senses, is interior. That is, the mind puts together the entire world from all the data presented by the senses. The images, etc. of the world are not 'out there' at all but mind-made. This aspect of Buddhist teaching both encourages one to practise Dharma and will be appreciated increasingly as one does so. While these two verses are not the only place where primacy of mind is insisted upon, the fact that they stand first in the Pāli Dhp. shows the esteem in which they were held.

Buddhists generally have given a high place to loving-kindness and helpfulness, notably of course, among Mahāyāna teachers of the Bodhisattva ideal. As illustration of this there are the Bodhisattva vows to take all beings across the ocean of birth and death, as I have quoted in the Four Great Vows above. In Mahāyāna, one should develop this bodhicitta – Awakened Heart – from the beginning of practice, Theravada emphasises, sometimes too strongly, that one should get oneself out of the swamp first and only then help others. This emphasis comes out very strongly in such verses as 158, 166 and 206–7. It should be remembered that these verses, like all those in this collection, were spoken by the Buddha to particular people at a certain time. They do not represent advice to all for every occasion.

Normally one would not connect this Dhp. with the Buddhist Tantras though in fact there are two or three verses which make such a connection, Verse 124 says:

"If a hand's without a wound
one may carry poison there -
unwounded poison enters not:
non-doers have no evil".

This sounds quite familiar to one who has learned doctrines of the Vajrayāna based on Buddhist Tantra. In the case of ordinary worldly people, those actions which usually increase greed, hatred and delusion are blamable and viewed karmically as poison. But for one who has dissolved the stains of greed, hatred and delusion, such a person does not have the karmic vision of those affected by the three poisons, though such a person may 'walk' among the poisons. When the wound of (I-making) is healed the three poisons do not enter the Awakened Heart.

The use of these poisons (empty in their nature) is a potent way to Awakening – but only if one has the proper empowerment from a great master and practises in such a way as not to break one's commitments to fellow practitioners and other living beings. In the Theravada context this verse is something of a puzzle and the story that is supposed to be the occasion for its utterance is unconvincing.

Verses 294–5 present an even stranger aspect. Slaying mother and father were said by the Buddha to be among the most heinous crimes leading the murderer to immediate hellish existence at the end of his or her life. How then can he teach that a person like this can be paragon? But here the Buddha speaks in what would later be called sandhyabhāsa – twilight language, the sort of words that convey a hidden meaning. While such presentations of Dharma are quite common in the Tantras they are scarcely found in the Pāli texts, still here is an example! Of course, it may be said that the Buddha intended to shock the hearers of these verses – and the commentarial story supports this – but this is precisely what the twilight language was for. Occasionally the Buddha in the Pāli tradition does use obscure similes which he later explains. These verses, being out of context, can only be clarified with the aid of the Commentary.

"Resplendent does the Buddha shine" says verse 387 and reminds us of the fact that it is not uncommon for practitioners to experience visions. The splendour of the Buddhas' radiance is indeed an important part of many Buddhist meditations in the Mahāyāna and Vajrayāna. Though Theravāda does not make much of such methods, they are both widespread and popular in Mahāyāna countries. In fact, the verse could almost be poetic brief description of many Tibetan painted scrolls – thankas used for meditation.

UPON THIS TRANSLATION

A few remarks need to be made about the present translation. First, it is in verse, rather than in prose as are most Dhp. translations in English. I have attempted the impossible, translating verse into verse from one language into another at the same time trying to preserve the meaning. I have aimed at poetic expression because I wanted the verses to be memorable. It is for readers to judge whether or not I have succeeded.

Second, non-sexist language has been used wherever this was possible though occasional 'he's' and 'him's' will still be found. English, particularly in verse-form, sometimes presents difficulties in this way which cannot be overcome.

Third, Sanskrit forms of Buddhist terms, rather than their Pāli equivalents, have been used throughout. Thus you will find: karma (not kamma), dharma (not dhamma), sūtra (not sutta) and nirvāna (not nibbāna). All such terms are adequately explained in the notes following each chapter.

Fourth, Dhp. verses are a mixture, some suitable for everyone whatever kind of life they lead and some really only referring to monks and nuns. When you encounter the latter verses, some of which have been noted, remember that their advice is only for those who have given up the household life for practice as monks and nuns.

Fifth, the title chosen is rather a poetic one, Jewels within the Heart. The ordinary use of the word Jewels is associated with display and adornments to enhance one's appearance. This title was chosen to remind us, that there are these brilliant and incomparable Jewels of Truth within the Hearts of all of us. A literal translation would be Verses on the Truth, Path or Law.

In bringing to a close this work stretching over several years, I should like to dedicate whatever merits it has to my parents, my Teachers in Dharma, to all my kind supporters and friends and to all sentient beings generally that their sufferings may be allayed, their happiness increase, their lives be long and fruitful and their hearts be at peace. May this insignificant contribution to the spread of the True Dharma help sentient beings towards the Incomparable Perfect Enlightenment.

I
YAMAKAVAGGA
VERSES ON THE PAIRS

1.   Dharmas are forerun by mind,
   mind's their chief, mind-made are they;
   if with a corrupted mind
   one should either speak or act
   dukkha follows caused by that,
   as wheel does on the ox's hoof.   (1)

2.   Dharmas are forerun by mind,
   mind's their chief, mind-made are they;
   if with a clearly confident mind
   one should either speak or act,
   happiness follows caused by that,
   as one's shadow follows after.   (2)

3.   Who bear within them enmity:
   'He has abused and beaten me,
   defeated me and plundered me',
   hate is not allayed for them.   (3)

4.   Who bear within no enmity:
   'He has abused and beaten me,
   defeated me and plundered me',
   hate is quite allayed for them.   (4)

1

5. Never here by enmity
    are those with enmity allayed:
    they are allayed by amity –
    this is the Natural Law.   (5)

6. Still others do not understand
    that we must perish in this world:
    those who understand this,
    their quarrels are allayed.   (6)

7. One who beauty contemplates,
    whose faculties are unrestrained,
    in food no moderation knows,
    is languid, who is indolent:
    that one does Mara overthrow,
    as wind a tree of little strength.   (7)

8. One who foulness contemplates,
    whose faculties are well-restrained,
    in food does moderation know,
    is full of faith, who's diligent:
    that one no Mara overthrows,
    as wind does not a rocky mount.   (8)

9. One who wears the stainless robe
    who's yet not free from stain,
    without restraint and truthfulness,
    for the stainless robe's unworthy.   (9)

10. But one who's purified of stains,
    in moral conduct firmly set,
    having restraint and truthfulness –
    is worthy of stainless robe.   (10)

11. The real imagined in unreality
     while seeing unreal as truly real;
     roaming fields of ill-directed thought
     never they to the real arrive.   (11)

12. That which is real they know as real,
     and the unreal to be unreal;
     roaming fields of well-directed thought
     they do to the real arrive.   (12)

13. Even as rain penetrates
     a dwelling thinly thatched,
     likewise lust penetrates
     a mind uncultivated.   (13)

14. As rain never penetrates
     a house completely thatched,
     so lust never penetrates
     a mind well cultivated.   (14)

15. Here one grieves, one grieves hereafter,
     in both wise does the evil-doer grieve;
     one grieves and is afflicted
     one's own base karmas seeing.   (15)

16. Here one joys, one joys hereafter;
     in both wise does the merit-maker joy;
     one joys and rejoices,
     one's own pure karmas seeing.   (16)

17. Here one burns one burns hereafter,
     in both wise does the evil-doer burn;

'Evil have I done' – remorsefully one burns,
and more one burns gone to woeful states.(17)

18.   Here one's glad and glad hereafter,
in both wise is the merit-maker glad;
'Merit have I made' – serenely one is glad,
and more one's glad gone to blissful states.(18)

19.   Though oft reciting sacred words
a heedless one's no practicer,
as a cowherd counting others' kine –
in peacefulness one has no share.   (19)

20.   Though little reciting sacred words
truly the Dharma one practises:
clear of delusion, greed and hate,
wisdom perfected, heart well-freed,
one clings not here nor clings hereafter –
in peacefulness one has a share.   (20)

NOTES

Numbers refer to verse-numbers in the chapter.

1. **Dukkha** – usually not translated in this book but in one or two places rendered by 'ill'. Means all kinds of unsatisfactory, painful or frustrating experience, from great physical and mental suffering to very subtle dissatisfaction with all experiences, which are impermanent, liable to deterioration and passing away, and empty of self.

5. **Dharma** – here meaning a Law true at all times.

7.–8. **Mara** – all sorts of obstacles to Dharma-practice, such as defilements of the mind, the instability of all conditioned things, death – also a personification of these as a Tempter.

8. **Foulness** – asubha – lit., the non-attractive, not beautiful, means the body looked at as it is made up of the 32 parts, beginning "head-hair, body-hair, nails, teeth, skin, …", or as a corpse in the stages of decay, as it will be. See 349–350.

9.–10. **Stain-robe** – this is a pun in Pali on these two words, which cannot be reproduced in English.

15.–18. **Both wise** – in this world (here) and the next life (hereafter).

15.–16. **Karmas** – means intentional actions or volitions. It does not mean 'fate' (which is a non-buddhist way of thinking) nor the fruits or results of karma.

17. **He burns** – also translated 'he suffers' and by extension 'remorsefully'.

17. **Woeful states** – States of existence inferior (in happiness and intelligence) to human beings, such as animals, hungry ghosts and hell-wraiths (q.v. Ch. XXII). See notes to verse 44.

18. **Merit** – puñña, good karma by mind, speech or body which "cleanses and purifies the heart of the doer". Merit is a poor translation therefore.

18. **Blissful States** – States of existence superior (in happiness, subtleness of body, length of life, and sometimes of knowledge) to human beings, such as the various heavenly planes in the realms of desire, subtle form and formlessness. But the devas (gods) who inhabit them are not Enlightened and may have wrong views. See notes to verse 44.

20. **Here or Hereafter** – This world or the next.

II
APPAMĀDAVAGGA
VERSES ON HEEDFULNESS

1. Heedfulness – the Deathless Path,
    heedlessness – the path to death:
    those who are heedful do not die,
    heedless ones are like the dead.   (21)

2. The wise, then, recognising this
    as the distinction of heedfulness,
    pleased with the sphere of Noble Ones
    in heedfulness rejoice.   (22)

3. They meditate persistently,
    constantly they firmly strive;
    the steadfast to Nirvana reach,
    the Unexcelled Secure from bonds.   (23)

4. Assiduous and mindful
    pure karma making and considerate,
    restrained, by Dharma living,
    for such a one fame grows.   (24)

5. By energy and heedfulness
    by taming and by self-control,
    that one who's wise should make an isle
    no flood can overwhelm.   (25)

6. Foolish folk of little wit
    indulge in heedlessness:
    one who's wise guards heedfulness
    like the greatest wealth.   (26)

7. Don't indulge in heedlessness!
    Be not obsessed with sex!
    The heedful and contemplative
    attains abundant bliss.   (27)

8. When a wise one drives away
    heedlessness by heedfulness,
    having ascended wisdom's tower
    steadfast, one surveys the fools,
    griefless, views the grieving folk,
    as mountaineer does those below.   (28)

9. Among the heedless, heedful,
    among the sleepy, wide awake.
    As thoroughbred outruns a hack
    so one of good wisdom goes.   (29)

10. Heedfulness is always praised,
    heedlessness is ever blamed,
    By heedfulness did Magha go
    to the lordship of the gods.   (30)

11. The bhikkhu liking heedfulness,
    seeing fear in heedlessness,
    advances as a conflagration
    burning fetters great and small.   (31)

12. The bhikkhu liking heedfulness,
     seeing fear in heedlessness,
     never will he fall away –
     near he is to Nirvana.   (32)

NOTES

1. **Heedfulness** – appamāda – lit. non-laziness, non intoxication, an important term covering mindfulness, wisdom and effort.

1. **Deathless** – amata – another term for Nirvana that which is not born and so is not subject to passing away. It does not mean the eternal existence in a heaven, as believed in by some religions.

2. **Sphere of Noble Ones** – the Pure Abodes, which are 5 planes in the Brahma-world or realm of subtle form, where people who have become Non-returners (to human birth) have a last blissful existence. Ariyas (meaning Nobles) are those people who realize the Truth of Dharma in their own hearts.

3. **Nirvana** – the ultimate goal of Buddhists, the cutting off of all defilements, passions and fetters, and so the end of the round of birth and death and of all dukkha – perfect happiness and peace beyond all conceptions of self. "The unexcelled Secure from bonds" is another term for Nirvana.

4. **Mindful** – of the body, feelings, mental states and mental factors as taught in the Buddha's Discourse on the Establishment of Mindfulness.

10. **Magha** – name of a prince who had made much merit by looking after others' welfare and so was born in the next life as Sakka, ruler of the devas, or gods.

11. **Bhikkhu** – Buddhist monk who has been ordained according to procedures laid down by the Buddha and who leads a celibate life, as well as studying and practising Dharma and trying to realize it in himself.

11. **Fetters** – saṁyojana – 10 of them: the great fetters are – the view identifying body and mind as 'I' or 'mine', uncertainty, attachment to vows and ceremonies as the essence of religion, sensual desire, hatred; while the small or fine ones are – desire for birth in the realm of subtle form, desire for birth in the formless realm, conceit, restlessness, and unknowing (of the Four Noble Truths, see 188–192).

III
CITTAVAGGA
VERSES ON THE MIND

1. The swaying wavering mind
   hard to guard and hard to check,
   one of wisdom renders straight
   as fletcher does a shaft.   (33)

2. As fish from its watery home
   is drawn and cast upon the land,
   even so flounders this mind:
   while Mara's realm abandoning.   (34)

3. The mind is very hard to check
   and swift, it falls on what it wants.
   The training of the mind is good,
   a mind so tamed brings happiness.   (35)

4. The mind is very hard to see
   and fine, it falls on what it wants.
   One who's wise should guard the mind,
   a guarded mind brings happiness.   (36)

5. Faring far, wandering alone,
   formless and lying in a cave –
   this mind, who do restrain it
   are freed from Mara's bonds.   (37)

6. One of unsteady mind,
    who doesn't know True Dharma,
    who is of wavering confidence
    full wisdom fails to win.   (38)

7. One of unflooded mind,
    a mind that is not battered,
    abandoning evil, merit too,
    for one Awake there is no fear.   (39)

8. One having known this urn-like body,
    firmed this mind as fortress town,
    fought Mara with the wisdom-sword
    will guard those gains, be unattached.   (40)

9. Not long alas – and it will lie
    this body here, upon the earth!
    Discarded, void of consciousness
    and useless as a rotten log.   (41)

10. Whatever foe may do to foe,
    or hater those they hate,
    the ill-directed mind indeed
    can do one greater harm.   (42)

11. Neither mother nor father too
    nor any other relative can do,
    such good as can be done to one
    by well-directed mind.   (43)

NOTES

2.   **Mara's realm** – the range of all conditioned things: The eye and sight objects, the ear and sounds, the nose and smells, the tongue and tastes, the body and touches, the mind and thought objects.

5.   **Faring far ... cave** – faring far because the mind can range through past, present and future, the existent and the non-existent, etc.; wandering alone because no two thought moments arise at one time; formless because the mind (= feeling, recognition, mental formations [thoughts, etc.] and consciousness) is immaterial and not to be confused with the brain; lying in a cave because the undisturbed and pure mind naturally tends to Awakening.

7.   **Unflooded mind** – not soaked or wetted by lust, desire.

7.   **A mind ... not battered** – not assaulted by hatred, anger.

7.   **Awake** – always alert and so free from fears born of defilements, not as most people who are afflicted by defilements and so slothful, even though their bodies are awake.

IV
PUPPHAVAGGA
VERSES ON FLOWERS

1. Who will comprehend this earth,
   the underworlds and realms divine?
   Who choose the well-taught Dharma-way
   as skilled florist a flower?   (44)

2. One who's trained will comprehend
   this earth and worlds above, below.
   He'll choose the well-taught Dharma-way
   as skilled florist a flower.   (45)

3. This foam-like body having known
   and woken to its mirage state
   smashing Mara's flowered shafts
   unseen beyond the Death-king go.   (46)

4. For one who has a clinging mind
   and gathers only pleasure-blooms
   Death does seize and carry away,
   as great flood a sleeping village.   (47)

5. For one of desires insatiate
   who gathers only pleasure-blooms
   for one who has a clinging mind
   the Ender overcomes.   (48)

6. As bee goes to a flower,
    harms there neither hue nor scent
    but gathers nectar, flies away,
    so in town One Wise behaves.   (49)

7. Not others' opposition,
    nor what they did or failed to do,
    but in oneself should be sought
    things done, things left undone.   (50)

8. As a bloom many-hued
    beautiful though unperfumed,
    so, fruitless the well-spoken words
    of one who does not act.   (51)

9. Just as bloom many-hued,
    beautiful and perfumed too,
    so, fruitful the well-spoken words
    of one who acts as well.   (52)

10. As from a mass of flowers
    many a garland may be made,
    so by one born mortal
    should many good deeds be done.   (53)

11. The fragrance of flowers goes not
            against the wind,
    neither that of sandalwood, jasmine
            or lavender,
    but the fragrance of virtue counters
            the wind,
    all-pervasive is virtue of the good.   (54)

12. Sandalwood or lavender,
    lotus or the jasmine great –
    of these many fragrances
    virtue's fragrance is the best.   (55)

13. Faint is this fragrance
    of lavender and sandalwood,
    best is fragrance of the good
    which soars amongst the gods.   (56)

14. Those with perfect virtue
    who live with heedfulness,
    freed by Final Knowledge
    Mara never finds their path.   (57)

15. As beside the highroad
    where rubbish in a pit is flung
    there flourishes the lotus bloom
    fragrant and the mind's delight –   (58)

16. So among rubbish-beings –
    common humans blind-become,
    the Perfect Buddha's pupil
    outshines with wisdom bright.   (59)

NOTES

1. **This earth** – oneself, to know oneself thoroughly.
1. **The under worlds** – these are the states of woe, such as the hungry ghosts (born so because meanness and attachment when men), the animals (born so because of thinking only of animal pleasures when men), and hell-wraiths (born so because of cruelty when men). None of these states are permanent.

1. **Divine** – lit. 'shining ones', the gods who arise in those heavenly planes because having made good karma when human. There are many planes of increasing subtlety and tranquillity. No type of existence, human, woeful or blissful, is permanent.

2. **One trained** – a Noble One who has seen Dharma directly.

3. **Mara's flowered shafts** – sensual pleasures called 'flower tipped' because alluring.

3. **Death-King** – Māra, one meaning of which is death.

5. **Ender** – Māra, death again.

6. **One Wise** – a muni, also one who is silent or practises silence, as bhikkhus are when they collect alms-food in a village. But he and other enlightened practitioners are called munis, because they are silent inside, without proliferation of thought. Sakyamuni, the Sage of the Sakya people, is one of the epithets of the Buddha.

8. **Does not act** – that is, in accord with his words.

11. **Lavender** – lit. Tagara – a fragrant bush used for making incense.

10. **Pupil** – lit. 'one who hearkens' – anyone who has heard the Dharma is a hearkener, but those who have hearkened to such good effect that they have at least glimpsed Nirvana, are called Noble Hearkeners which is the meaning here.

V
BALAVAGGA
VERSES ON THE FOOL

1. Long is the night for one awake,
    long the league for the weary one,
    the wandering-on is long for fools
    who know not Dharma True.   (60)

2. If a wayfarer fails to find
    one better or one equal,
    steadfast, then fare on alone
    for with a fool's no fellowship.   (61)

3. 'Sons have I, wealth have I' –
    thus the fool frets:
    he himself is not his own,
    how then are sons, how wealth?   (62)

4. Conceiving so his foolishness
    the fool is thereby wise:
    while 'fool' is called that fool
    conceited that he's wise.   (63)

5. Though all through life the fool
    might wait upon the wise,
    no more Dharma can he discern
    than spoon the taste of soup.   (64)

6. Though briefly one intelligent
    might wait upon the wise,
    quickly Dharma he discerns
    as tongue the taste of soup.   (65)

7. Fools of feeble wisdom fare
    enemies to themselves,
    making evil karma
    which is of bitter fruit.   (66)

8. That karma's not well made
    from which there is remorse,
    of which one senses the result
    with weeping and a tear-stained face. (67)

9. But well made is that karma
    which done brings no remorse,
    of which one senses the result
    with gladness and with joy.   (68)

10. 'As sweet as honey' thinks the fool
    so long the evil is unripe,
    but when the evil ripens
    then to the fool comes dukkha.   (69)

11. Month after month with blady-grass tip
    a fool might eat his food:
    he's not worth a sixteenth part
    of one who Dharma knows.   (70)

12. The evil karma done, like milk,
    does not at once turn sour.

17

    Smouldering does it follows the fool
    like fire with ashes covered.   (71)

13.   Truly to his detriment
    skill is born to the fool:
    ruined his better nature
    and scattered are his wits.   (72)

14.   'Among monks precedence
    in monasteries authority,
    from other families honour',
    so for status fools will wish.   (73)

15.   Let both monks and laity think:
    'This was done by me;
    whatever the works, great and small,
    let them depend on me'.
    Such intention of a fool
    swells his greed and his conceit.   (74)

16.   One is the way to worldly gain,
    another to Nirvana leads.
    Clearly comprehending this
    the monk or Buddha's follower,
    should take no joy in praise and gain
    but dwell content in solitude.   (75)

NOTES

1. **The wandering-on** – saṃsāra – the wandering in purposeless fashion from life to life without Dharma direction.

1. **Dharma True** – saddhamma – Dharma which is True because discovered in the Awakening or Enlightenment (bodhi) of the Buddha, and leading the practitioner of it to Enlightenment.

2. **Wayfarer** – one who practises a spiritual path. The verse refers to finding a good teacher or companion (see 76–77). A fool is a weak person who makes unwholesome karma.

11. **Blady-grass tip** – some Indian ascetics used blades of a sharp, cutting grass as a painful way of eating very little food. The Buddha taught the uselessness of such extreme asceticism.

13. **Scattered are his wits** – lit. 'his head is cleft apart' – his understanding is destroyed.

VI
PAṆḌITAVAGGA
VERSES ON THE WISE

1. Should one meet a person wise
   who points out faults and censures them
   thereby laying treasures bare,
   with such a sage should one consort.
   Consorting so one is enriched,
   goes never to decline.   (76)

2. Let him then exhort, instruct
   and check one from all evil things:
   true pupils hold him dear,
   not dear is he to the false.   (77)

3. Don't go around with evil friends
   with rogues do not consort.
   Spend your time with noble friends
   with worthy ones consort.   (78)

4. Who Dharma drinks has joy
   with a clear and tranquil heart;
   one so wise ever delights
   in Dharma declared by Noble Ones.   (79)

5. Irrigators lead the waters,
   fletchers bend the shafts,

as joiners shape their timber:
wise ones tame themselves. (80)

6.   Just as a mighty boulder
shakes not with the wind,
so the wise are never moved
either by praise or blame. (81)

7.   Just like the deepest lake,
a lake so calm and clear,
so the Dharmas having heard –
serene the wise become. (82)

8.   Everything the good renounce
the peaceful chatter not of fond delights,
and whether touched by pleasure or pain,
nor joy nor woe in the wise is seen. (83)

9.   Neither for one's own, nor for another's sake
should one wish for children, wealth, estate,
nor success desire by means unjust:
thus virtuous and wise, righteous one
would be. (84)

10.   Among folk they are few
who go to the Further Shore,
most among humanity
scurry on this hither shore. (85)

11.   But who the well-taught Dharma do,
their Dharma according with Dharma,
from Death's dominion hard to leave
they'll cross to the Further Shore. (86)

12.   Abandoning the Dharmas dark
     the wise should cultivate the bright;
     having from home to homeless gone
     in solitude unsettling –   (87)

13.   Let them desire that rare delight,
     renouncing pleasures, owning nought;
     those wise ones should cleanse themselves
     from all defilement of the mind.   (88)

14.   Those who come to Wakening
     with mind full-cultivated
     delight, no longer clinging,
     in relinquishing attachment,
     they, unstained and radiant
     in this world have reached Nirvana.   (89)

NOTES

1. **Never to decline** – a literal rendering of this line is 'better it is, never for worse'.

7. **Dharmas** – the different ways of training people.

10. **The Further Shore** – there are two shores: the hither shore, where most people are now, of fear and danger, defilements and dukkha, birth and death, and the further shore – another name for Nirvana where none of these exist.

11. **Their Dharma according with Dharma** – the way that they do or practise their Dharma so that it accords with the ultimate Dharma – Dharmakāya – beyond all descriptions.

12. **The Dharmas dark ... bright** – the dark are the ten pathways of evil karma: killing living creatures, taking what is not given, wrong conduct in sexual relations, false speech, slanderous speech, harsh speech, nonsensical chatter, covetousness, ill-will, and wrong views. The bright Dharmas are the opposite of them.

12. **Home to homeless** – the phrase 'going forth from home to homeless' means leaving the life of householders and taking up the life of a homeless practitioner. See 184, 195.

VII
ARAHATAVAGGA
VERSES ON THE ARAHAT

1. With journey finished and sorrowless,
   from everything completely free;
   for one who's loosened all the ties
   passions' fever is not found.   (90)

2. Mindful ones exert themselves,
   in no abode do they delight,
   as swans abandoning their lake,
   home after home they leave behind.   (91)

3. For those who don't accumulate,
   who well reflect upon their food,
   have as range the nameless and
   the void of perfect freedom too:
   such 'going' is as hard to trace
   as birds that wing through space.   (92)

4. For whom pollutions are destroyed,
   who's unattached to nutriment,
   who has as range the nameless and
   the void of perfect freedom too;
   such path indeed is hard to trace
   as birds that wing through space.   (93)

5.   Whose faculties are pacified
       as steeds by charioteer well-tamed,
       pride abandoned, unpolluted,
       to even devas 'Such' is dear.   (94)

6.   Like earth is one who's well-behaved
       and 'Such' and not resentful;
       like city post, like filth-free lake:
       no wanderings-on for 'Such' a one.   (95)

7.   Peaceful his mind and peaceful
       his speech and action too,
       perfect in knowledge of freedom,
       one 'Such' is of utmost peace.   (96)

8.   Beyond beliefs, the Unmade known,
       with fetters finally severed,
       with karmas cut and cravings shed,
       supreme among people are they.   (97)

9.   Whether in town or woods,
       whether in vale, on hill,
       wherever dwell the Arahants
       delightful is that place.   (98)

10.   Delightful are the forests
       where folk do not delight,
       there the passionless do delight –
       for they're not pleasure-seekers.   (99)

NOTES

3. **Accumulate** – 2 accumulations: of the 4 necessities – clothes, food, shelter and medicines – and of karma. There is usually attachment to the first, while the second ensures that one will stay in the round of birth and death.

3.–4. **Nameless ... void ... perfect freedom** – Nirvana is perfect freedom because free from defilements and the dukkha they cause. It is also the void because empty of the self-idea, and nameless because it has no 'signs' which can be conceptualised.

4. **Pollutions** – āsava – that which flows into the mind-heart defiling it.

4. **Nutriments** – āhara – 4 kinds: Material food for the body; contact (of senses with sense-objects) nutriment for the feelings (pleasant, painful, neutral); mental volitional nutriment (=karma) for rebirth; and consciousness-nutriment for mind and body at the moment of conception.

5. **'Such'** – tadi – one who knows things as they really are; who has direct perception of reality all the time.

6. **Wandering on** – saṁsāra. See 60.

8. **Beyond beliefs** – because knowing directly for oneself.

8. **Unmade** – another term for Nirvana which is not created.

8. **With karmas cut** – lit. 'occasion's destroyer' – one who has destroyed all occasions for doing either good or evil with the self idea.

VIII
SAHASSAVAGGA
VERSES ON THOUSANDS

1. Though a thousand speeches be
    composed of meaningless lines,
    better the one that's meaningful
    hearing which there's peace.   (100)

2. Though a thousand verses be
    composed of meaningless lines,
    better the single meaningful verse
    hearing which there's peace.   (101)

3. Though chanting a hundred verses
    composed of meaningless lines,
    better the single Dharma verse
    hearing which there's peace.   (102)

4. Though a thousand times a thousand
    in battle one may conquer,
    yet should one conquer just oneself
    one is the greatest conqueror.   (103)

5. Greater the conquest of oneself
    than subjugating others,
    that one who's always well-restrained
    that person tamed of self –   (104)

6. Neither deva nor minstrel divine,
    nor Mara together with Brahma,
    can overthrow the victory
    of such a one as this.   (105)

7. Month by month for a hundred years
    a thousand one might sacrifice:
    but if for a single second one
    did honour the self-developed,
    such honour then were better by far
    than a century of sacrifice.   (106)

8. One might tend for a hundred years
    the forest's sacred fire,
    but if for a single second one
    did honour the self-developed,
    such honour then were better by far
    than a century of sacrifice.   (107)

9. Whatever one who merit seeks
    should for a year make sacrifice,
    all comes not to a quarter part
    of honouring the Straight.   (108)

10. For one of respectful nature
    who ever the elders honours,
    long life and beauty, joy and strength,
    these qualities increase.   (109)

11. Though one should live a hundred years
    immoral, uncontrolled,
    yet better is life for a single day
    moral, meditative.   (110)

12. Though one should live a hundred years
foolish, uncontrolled,
yet better is life for a single day
wise and meditative. (111)

13. Though one should live a hundred years
lazy, of little effort,
yet better is life for a single day
making steady effort. (112)

14. Though one should live a hundred years
not seeing rise and fall,
yet better is life for a single day
seeing rise and fall. (113)

15. Though one should live a hundred years
not seeing the Deathless State,
yet better is life for a single day
seeing the Deathless State. (114)

16. Though one should live a hundred years
not seeing Dharma supreme,
yet better is life for a single day
seeing Dharma supreme. (115)

NOTES

6. **Minstrel divine** – gandharva, a class of devas skilled in music.

6. **Brahmā** – the ruler of the worlds of Brahma in the realm of subtle form, as Māra is ruler over the realm of sense-desire.

9. **The Straight** – Noble Ones are so called, because of having rid themselves of the crookedness of some or all defilements.

14. **Rise and fall** – Seeing the momentary arising and passing away of mind and body.

16. **Dharma supreme** – Liberation from all conditioned existence.

IX
PĀPAVAGGA
VERSES ON EVIL

1. Make haste towards the good
   and check the mind from evil,
   the one who's slow to merit make
   delights the mind in evil.   (116)

2. If one should some evil do
   then do it not again, again;
   do not wish for it anew
   for evil grows to pain.   (117)

3. If one should some merit make
   do it then again and again;
   one should wish for it anew
   for merit grows to joy.   (118)

4. Even one evil goodness knows
   as long as evil ripens not,
   but when the evil ripens
   then one evil evil knows.   (119)

5. Even the virtuous evil knows
   as long as virtue ripens not,
   but when the virtue ripens
   then the virtuous virtue knows.   (120)

6. Think lightly not of evil:
    'It will not come to me' –
    for by the falling of water drops
    a water jar is filled:
    fools with evil fill themselves
    gathering little by little.   (121)

7. Think lightly not of merit:
    'It will not come to me' –
    for by the falling of water drops
    a water jar is filled:
    the wise with merit fill themselves
    gathering little by little.   (122)

8. As merchant on a perilous path
    wealth possessing but little guard,
    as life-loving person with poison –
    so evils should be shunned.   (123)

9. If a hand's without a wound
    one may carry poison there –
    unwounded, poison enters not:
    non-doers have no evil.   (124)

10. Whoso offends an inoffensive man,
    one who's innocent and blameless,
    upon that fool evil falls
    as fine dust flung against the wind   (125)

11. Some are born in wombs,
    those of evil deeds in hell,
    good-farers to the heavens go,
    the unpolluted wholly cool.   (126)

12. Neither in the sky, nor surrounded by sea,
    nor by entering a cavern in the hills,
    nowhere is found that place upon the
        earth
    where one would be from evil karma
        free. (127)

13. Neither in the sky, nor surrounded by sea,
    nor by entering a cavern in the hills,
    nowhere is found that place upon the
        earth
    where one would not be overcome by
        death. (128)

NOTES

4.-5. A person living an evil life may be happy and comfortable, the happiness being the result of past good karma. Only when his evil karma begins to fruit does he experience dukkha. The opposite is true of the good person. (see 69, 71)

9. As poison may be carried in an unwounded hand so what are usually called greed, hatred and delusion may be used by one who has no evil intention. Only those whose practice of Dharma has matured will be able to do this.

11. **Womb** – mammals, including human beings; hell, heavens – birth is spontaneous in these states without need for parents. Ghosts are also spontaneously born. The un-polluted, the Awakened have literally 'nibbān-ed' which means neither existence nor non-existence. To translate with another verb, for example: "The Undefiled Ones pass away into Nibbāna", distorts the meaning as Nibbāna is not a place, and therefore cannot be gone to.

12. **Evil karma** – one could not find a place to avoid the fruits or results of evil karma.

X
DANDAVAGGA
VERSES ON FORCE

1. All tremble at force!
    All are afraid of death!
    Likening others to oneself
    kill not nor cause to kill   (129)

2. All tremble at force!
    Life is dear to all!
    Likening others to oneself
    kill not nor cause to kill   (130)

3. Whoever harms with force
    beings desiring happiness,
    as seeker after happiness
    one gains no future joy.   (131)

4. Whoever doesn't harm with force
    beings desiring happiness,
    as seeker after happiness
    one then gains future joy.   (132)

5. To others speak not harshly
    speaking so, they may retort.
    Dukkha indeed is quarrelsome speech
    and force for force may hurt you.   (133)

6. If as a broken gong
    never you reverberate,
    quarrelling's not part of you:
    that Nirvana's reached.   (134)

7. As with force the cowherds drive
    their cattle out to graze,
    like this decay and death drive out
    the life from beings all.   (135)

8. When the fool does evil deeds
    their end he does not know.
    Such karma burns the one unwise
    as one who's scorched by fire.   (136)

9. Whoever forces the forceless
    or offends the inoffensive
    speedily comes indeed
    to one of these ten states: (137)

10. Sharp pain or deprivation,
    or injury to the body,
    or to a serious disease,
    derangement of the mind;   (138)

11. Troubled by the government,
    or else false accusation,
    or the loss of relatives,
    destruction of one's wealth;   (139)

12. Or one's houses burn
    in raging conflagration,

at the body's end, in hell
arises that unwise one. (140)

13.   Neither going naked, nor matted hair,
                nor filth,
        nor fasting nor sleeping on the earth,
        no penance on the heels, nor sweatiness,
                nor grime,
        can purify a mortal still overcome
                by doubt. (141)

14.   Even though adorned, if living at peace,
        calm, tamed and sure a practitioner pure,
        with force laid aside for all sorts of beings –
        priest is he, monk is he, bhikkhu is he! (142)

15.   Where in the world is found
        that one restrained by shame
        awakened out of sleep,
        as splendid horse with whip? (143)

16.   As a splendid horse touched with whip
        ardent becomes, is deeply moved:
        so by faith and virtue, effort too,
        by meditation, Dharma-trial,
        by knowledge, kindness, mindfulness,
        abandon dukkha limitless. (144)

17.   Irrigators lead the waters,
        fletchers bend the shafts,
        as joiners shape their timber:
        the well-conducted tame themselves. (145)

NOTES

1. **Force** – dands, lit. a 'staff' or 'rod', hence a 'weapon' and by extension 'punishment' but neither this nor the literal meaning fit in all the verses. 'Blows' is appropriate in some places, but 'force' seems to fit best as a general translation.

3.-4. **Future** – lit. 'hereafter' – the next life or future lives.

6. **Nirvana** – even though Nirvana has not yet been attained, yet it is as though one had attained it if one acts in this way.

13. All these actions are the austerities (tapas) used by Indian yogis down to the present day. They are ineffective for controlling the mind.

14. **Practitioner pure** – one who lives a pure life, usually a celibate life.

14. **Priest ... monk ... bhikkhu ...** – a brahmin in Hindu usage means one of the brahmin caste and perhaps a priest, but the Buddha used this exalted word for an Awakened One and defined it (388) as one who 'bars out badness'. See also 393, 396. A samana who 'lives serene' (388) usually means a homeless religious wanderer. See also 264–5. A bhikkhu (from root bhik – to beg) is a mendicant monk, but see the Buddha's remarks about a true bhikkhu in Ch. XXV, and 266–7. This verse was spoken about a king's minister and plainly shows the Buddha's estimation of who is really a monk. Practitioners of Dharma should not be thought of as restricted to those in robes.

16. **Knowledge, kindness** – the perfect combination of wisdom and compassion, third among the nine qualities of the Buddha.

17. See also, 80.

XI
JARĀVAGGA
VERSES ON DECAY

1. Why this laughter, why this joy,
   when it's ever blazing?
   shrouded all about by gloom
   won't you look for light? (146)

2. See this body beautiful,
   a mass of sores, a congeries,
   much considered but miserable
   where nothing's stable, nothing persists. (147)

3. All decrepit is this body,
   diseases' nest and frail;
   this foul mass is broken up –
   indeed life ends in death. (148)

4. These dove-hued bones
   scattered in fall
   like long white gourds –
   what joy in seeing them? (149)

5. This city's made of bones
   plastered with flesh and blood,
   within are stored decay and death,
   blaming others and conceit. (150)

6. Even rich royal chariots rot,
    the body also goes to decay;
    but the True Dharma doesn't decay
    so the True make it known to the calm. (151)

7. Just as the ox grows old
    so this man of little learning:
    his fleshiness increases,
    his wisdom waxes not.   (152)

8. Through many wandering births
    I hastened seeking, finding not
    the maker of this house –
    pain is birth again, again.   (153)

9. O maker of this house, you're seen!
    you shall not make a house again;
    all your beams have given way,
    rafters of the ridge decayed,
    mind to the Unconditioned gone,
    craving's exhaustion it has reached.   (154)

10. Who have not led the holy life
    or riches won while young,
    they linger on as aged cranes
    around a fished-out pond.   (155)

11. Who have not led the holy life
    or riches won while young,
    they lie around as worn-out bows
    sighing for the past.   (156)

NOTES

1.   **When it's ever blazing** – this world is blazing with the triple fires of greed, aversion and delusion.

6.   **The True** – the Buddha and his enlightened disciples. Their Dharma does not decay because founded on Enlightenment.

8-9   **Maker of this house** – this is a craving (taṇhā) and the house which it builds is this body. These two verses are said to be the first inspired words of the Buddha after his Enlightenment, words which were perhaps only thought, or if spoken aloud no one was present to hear them.

9.   **Unconditioned** – Nibbāna, which is unconditioned because not supported by or compounded of anything else.

10-11 **Holy life** – brahmacariya, the life of good Dharma practice. One should either, while young, succeed with the holy life or else make a success of the worldly life.

XII
ATTAVAGGA
VERSES ON ONESELF

1. If one holds oneself as dear,
    protected, one protects oneself,
    one who's wise should be aware
    through all the watches three.   (157)

2. Oneself should first establish
    oneself in what is proper,
    then others one may teach:
    and wise, one is not blamed.   (158)

3. As one teaches others
    so should one do oneself.
    Completely tamed, tame others then.
    Oneself to tame is hard!   (159)

4. Oneself is refuge of oneself-
    what else indeed could refuge be?
    By the good training of oneself
    one gains a refuge hard to gain.   (160)

5. By oneself is evil done,
    self-born and self produced,
    that evil grinds an unwise one
    as diamond hardest gem.   (161)

6. Whose conduct's very bad
   as oak tree strangled by ivy,
   so he does towards himself
   what enemies would wish. (162)

7. Incommendable deeds are easy to do
   and those not benefiting oneself:
   But commendable deeds and beneficial
   extremely hard are they to do. (163)

8. Whatever man unwise relies
   on evil view and so condemns
   the Teaching of the Arahats,
   or Noble Ones who Dharma live,
   he, as a bamboo fruiting,
   fruits to self-destruction. (164)

9. By oneself doing evil
   does one defile oneself,
   oneself not doing evil
   one purifies oneself;
   purity, impurity depend upon oneself,
   no one can purify another. (165)

10. Let none neglect their good
    for others' good however great:
    know well oneself's own good
    and to that good attend. (166)

NOTES

1.   **Protected** – this verse was spoken to a prince and his wife who were well-protected by their retainers, etc.

1.   **Watches three** – 3 watches of the night: 6–10 pm, 10 pm–2 am, 2–6 am.

2.   **Blamed** – lit. would not be defiled, that is, by the blame of others.

4.   **Refuge** – nātha, may also be translated 'protector, saviour, master, lord'. One is one's own saviour or protector. Even the great Bodhisattvas can only help when one makes an effort. See also 165.

6.   **Oak tree … ivy** – lit. sāla … māluva – the first is a fair, tall tree, but the second is a strangling creeper. The verse was spoken of Phra Devadatta, who, though a bhikkhu and the Buddha's cousin, three times tried to murder him, and caused schism in the Sangha.

10.   **Their good** – this verse emphasizes that awakening oneself is the most important aim in the Theravada teachings. However, it does not advocate selfishness which is never praised in any Buddhist teaching. Mahayana teachings of course stress that working with the good of a great number of other people *is* one's own good. These teachings have to be used at different stages of one's development.

XIII
LOKAVAGGA
VERSES ON THE WORLD

1. Do not follow base desires!
    nor live with heedlessness!
    Do not follow wrong beliefs
    or generate the world.   (167)

2. Rouse yourself, be diligent
    fare the well-faring Dharma;
    who fares in Dharma's happy
    in this world and the next.   (168)

3. Fare the well-faring Dharma,
    never by ill-faring fare;
    who fares in Dharma's happy
    in this world and the next.   (169)

4. Just as a bubble may be seen
    just as a faint mirage
    so should the world be viewed
    that the Death-king sees one not.   (170)

5. Come, do you observe this world
    compared to a rich, royal chariot,
    wherein fools settle down
    but alert ones have no bond.   (171)

6. Whoso was heedless formerly
    but later lives with heedfulness
    illumines all this world
    as moon when freed from clouds.   (172)

7. Who by wholesome karma
    covers up the evil done
    illumines all this world
    as moon when freed from clouds.   (173)

8. This world is blind-become,
    few are here who see within,
    as birds escaping from a net
    few go to heavenly realms.   (174)

9. Swans upon the sun's path fly,
    the powerful through space,
    conquering Mara and his host
    away from the world the wise are led.   (175)

10. One-Dharma disregarding –
    that falsely-speaking person –
    rejector of the other world:
    no evil's he'll not do.   (176)

11. Certainly to heavenly realms misers
               do not fare
    for never generosity is praised by fools,
    but one who's wise at generosity rejoices
    and happiness will have in future lives. (177)

12. Than o'er the earth sole sovereignty,
    than going to heavenly realms,

than Lordship over all the worlds:
better the Stream-winner's Fruit.   (178)

NOTES

1.   **Generate the world** – lit. 'be not a world-increaser' – that is, by repeated birth and death in it.

4-5   **So should the world be viewed** – compare with the famous Mahayana verse from the Diamond Sutra: "As stars, a fault of vision, or a lamp, illusion, rain-cloud or a bubble, a dream, a lightning-flash or dew-drop so the conditioned should be seen".

9.   **The powerful** – by means of mental development, various unusual abilities can be attained.

9.   **Māra and his host** – the 10 armies of Māra are: sensual pleasure, aversion to the holy life, hunger-thirst craving, mental-physical sloth, fear, uncertainty, detraction and obstinacy, gain, praise, fame, exalting oneself and despising others.

10.   **One-Dharma** – the fundamental law of truthfulness. The Buddha was called the Satyavadi – Truth-speaker and his teaching the Satya-dharma – the truthful teaching. Realization of the four Noble Truths (see 190–191) is the foundation of Awakening and for everyday restraint of living there is the fourth precept, to refrain from false speech.

12.   **Stream-winner's Fruit** – the first glimpse of Nirvana by one 'who has entered the stream' flowing to Enlightenment.

XIV
BUDDHAVAGGA
VERSES ON THE BUDDHA

1. His conquest not to be undone
   and those he's conquered cannot follow
       him:
   that Buddha traceless, of infinite range,
   then by which track will you trace him? (179)

2. In whom there's no entangling craving,
   and no ensnaring not anywhere leading:
   that Buddha traceless, of infinite range,
   then by which track will you trace him? (180)

3. Ever intent on meditation
   delighting in renunciation's peace;
   mindful, wise, the perfect Buddhas,
   to even devas they are dear.   (181)

4. Human birth is hard to gain,
   hard for mortals is their life,
   hard to hear the Dharma True,
   rare the arising of Buddhas.   (182)

5. Every evil never doing
   and in wholesomeness increasing

and one's heart well-purifying:
this is the Buddhas' Teaching. (183)

6.   'Penance supreme' is long-enduring
        patience,
'Nirvana is supreme' the Buddhas say
but one who kills is not a monk,
nor injurer an ordained one. (184)

7.   Not reviling, neither harming,
restrained to limit 'freedom's' ways,
moderation in one's food,
dwelling far in solitude,
and striving in the mind sublime:
this is the Buddhas' Teaching. (185)

8.   Not by rain of golden coins
is found desires' satiety:
desires are dukkha, of little joy –
thus a wise one understands. (186)

9.   Even with pleasures heavenly
that one finds no delight:
the perfect Buddha's pupil
delights in craving's end. (187)

10.   Many a 'refuge' do they seek
on hills, in woods, to sacred trees,
to monasteries and shrines they go,
folk by fear tormented. (188)

11.   Such 'refuges' are insecure
they are not supreme.

One's not free from dukkha
when to these 'refuges' gone.   (189)

12.   But going for refuge to Buddha,
      to Dharma and the Sangha too,
      one sees with perfect wisdom
      the tetrad of Noble Truths: (190)

13.   Dukkha, its causal arising
      the overcoming of dukkha,
      and the Noble Eightfold Path
      leading to dukkha's allaying.   (191)

14.   Such refuge is secure,
      such refuge is supreme,
      from all dukkha one is free,
      unto that refuge gone.   (192)

15.   Hard to find the pure and noble,
      who isn't born just anywhere,
      wherever one so wise is born
      that family thrives happily.   (193)

16.   Blessed is the birth of Buddhas,
      blest True Dharma's teaching,
      blest the Sangha's harmony,
      and blest their practice too.   (194)

17.   Who venerates the venerable –
      Buddhas or their hearkeners
      who've overcome the manifold,
      gone beyond grief and lamentation,   (195)

18. 'thus' are they, venerable,
     cool and free from every fear –
     no one's able to calculate
     their merit as 'just-so-much'.   (196)

NOTES

1. **Those he's conquered** – defilements destroyed at the moment of Enlightenment cannot arise again.

3. **Perfect Buddhas** – all who have awakened with or without teachers in the past, present, and future are called Buddha – Awake.

4. **Rare** – in Pali this is the same words as translated 'hard' three times already: 'hard is it to witness the arising of a Buddha'.

5. This verse is called 'The Heart of the Buddhas' Teachings': in the first line, restraint from evil karma; in the second, development of wholesome karma; in the third, the purification of one's heart with insight (vipassana) leading to wisdom (pañña) and Enlightenment (bodhi).

7. **Restrained to limit 'freedom's' ways** – lit. 'restrained by the Patimokkha'. However, the meaning of Patimokkha here is unclear. Often this word means the code of rules for monks (227 rules) or for nuns (311 rules). Here I translate as if the words was 'patimokkha' which PTS Dictionary defines as a medicine, 'against' (pati) 'the freedom' (mokkha), suggesting an anti-diarrhoeic, freedom being understood in the libertine sense.

12. **Refuge** – by 'Going-for-Refuge' to the Buddha, Dharma and Sangha, a person declares himself a Buddhist.

12-13 **Noble Truths** – ariyasacca, these are the teachings peculiar to the Buddhas for no one else has declared them completely. For a full exposition, see *The Word of the Buddha*, translated and compiled by Nyānatiloka Mahāthera (B.P.S. Kandy, Sri Lanka). See 273.

17. **The manifold** – papañca, here meaning the multiplicity and differentiation of things in the world, which permits the mind to wander through them expressing like and dislike. (See 253). In the next verse 'Thus' or 'Such' (tādi) is the overcoming of this (see 94–6), seeing things as they really are.

XV
SUKHAVAGGA
VERSES ON HAPPINESS

1. We the unhating live
   so happily midst the haters;
   among the hating humans
   from hatred dwell we free.   (197)

2. We who are healthy live
   so happily midst the unhealthy
   among unhealthy humans
   from ill-health dwell we free.   (198)

3. We the unfrenzied live
   so happily midst the frenzied
   among the frenzied humans
   from frenzy dwell we free.   (199)

4. We for whom there's nought;
   live indeed so happily,
   feeders on joy we'll be
   like resplendent gods.   (200)

5. Victory gives rise to hate,
   those defeated dwell in pain
   happily rest the Peaceful
   released from victory and defeat.   (201)

6. There's no fire like lust,
   no evil like aversion,
   no dukkha like the aggregates,
   no higher bliss than Peace. (202)

7. Hunger is the greatest ill,
   conditioned things, the greatest pain,
   knowing this really as it is –
   Nirvana bliss supreme. (203)

8. Health's the greatest gain
   contentment, best of wealth,
   trusting's best of kin,
   Nirvana bliss supreme. (204)

9. Having drunk of solitude
   and tasted Peace sublime,
   free from sorrow, evil-free
   one savours Dharma's joy. (205)

10. So fair's the sight of Noble Ones,
    ever good their company,
    by never seeing foolish men
    ever happy one may be. (206)

11. Who moves among fools' company
    must truly grieve for long,
    for ill the company of fools
    as ever that of foes:
    but weal a wise one's company
    as relatives together met. (207)

12.   So go with the steadfast, wise, well-versed,
      firm in virtue, practice-pure,
      ennobled, 'Such', who's sound, sincere,
      as moon in wake of Milky Way.   (208)

NOTES

1-3   These verses are said to have been spoken by the Buddha after he had stopped a war fought by his relatives over irrigation waters.

3.   By **'frenzied'** here is meant the worldly scramble for riches and power accompanied by the harming of others and thus by dissent and suffering: 'keeping up with the Jones' and surpassing them.

4.   **There's nought** – natthi kiñcanaṁ, nothing is 'owned' by one who is Enlightened as the ideas of 'owner' and 'ownership' are destroyed when the voidness of the 5 groups comprising 'oneself' is seen.

5.   **Victory and defeat** – a verse spoken about a king who had been defeated in battle. For the Buddhist attitude to victory see 103–105.

5–6   **Peaceful ... Peace ... Peace sublime** – (in 9) all refer to Nirvana and its experience.

6.   **Aggregates** – khandha, five constituents of personality: body, feeling, recognition, volitions, consciousness. They are all conditioned and so impermanent, dukkha and not-self. See next verse.

11.   **Ill** – dukkha, one of the few places where this has been translated. 'Weal' is elsewhere 'happiness' or 'bliss' (sukha).

XVI
PIYAVAGGA
VERSES ON THE DEAR

1. Seeking what should not be sought
   but seeking not what should be sought,
   one grasps the dear, forsakes the Search
   and envies those who seek. (209)

2. Don't with dear ones join
   nor those undear at any time;
   it's dukkha not to see the dear
   and seeing undear, dukkha too. (210)

3. So make not others dear
   for hard's the parting from them
   for whom there is no dear, undear,
   in them no bonds are found. (211)

4. From endearing grief is born,
   from endearing fear:
   one quite free of endearing
   has no grief – how fear? (212)

5. From affection grief is born,
   from affection fear:
   one quite free of affection
   has no grief – how fear: (213)

6. From lustfulness arises grief,
    from lustfulness springs fear:
    one wholly free of lustfulness
    has no grief – how fear?   (214)

7. From attachment grief is born,
    from attachment fear:
    one who is attachment-free
    has no grief-how fear?   (215)

8. Out of craving grief is born,
    out of craving fear:
    one quite free of craving
    has no grief – how fear?   (216)

9. Perfect in virtue and insight,
    firm in Dharma, knower of truth:
    dear to the people's such a one
    who does what should be done.   (217)

10. One with a wish for the Undeclared,
    with a mind exhilarated,
    a mind unbound from pleasures of sense,
    an 'upstream-goer's' called.   (218)

11. One who's long away from home
    returns in safety from afar,
    then friends, well-wishers,
            kinsmen too
    are overjoyed at his return.   (219)

12. In the same way the merit done
    when from this world to another gone

those merits then receive one there
as relatives a dear one come.   (220)

NOTES

1.   **Seeking ... sought ... seek** – translate all forms of the verbal root yunj which combines meanings like joining together and making effort. The best-known related word is 'yoga', a Pali and Sanskrit word which has a distant relative in the English word 'yoke'. This is a difficult verse to translate.

2-3   **Dear ... undear** – not easy to practise this in the household life but not impossible.

7.   **Attachment** – this means, love with selfishness, which is sure to bring grief and fear.

9.   **Does what should be done** – a practitioner should grow in moral conduct, meditation and wisdom.

10.   **The Undeclared** – another term for Nirvana, so called because one cannot declare where it exists, when it arose, what it looks like, etc.

10.   **An upstream-goer** – one who goes against the stream of worldly attachment.

XVII
KODHAVAGGA
VERSES ON ANGER

1.   Anger and pride should one forsake,
      all fetters cast aside
      dukkha's none where no desire,
      no binding to body or mind.   (221)

2.   Who, as a rolling chariot,
      can check arisen anger –
      him I call a charioteer,
      others merely hold the reins.   (222)

3.   Anger conquer by amity
      evil conquer with good,
      by giving conquer the miserly,
      liars conquer by truth.   (223)

4.   Speak truth and be not angry,
      from little give to one who asks:
      by these conditions three to go
      to presence of the gods.   (224)

5.   Those inoffensive sages
      in body e'er restrained
      go to the Everlasting State
      where gone they grieve no more.   (225)

6.   For the ever-vigilant
who train by night and day,
upon Nirvana ever intent,
pollutions fade away.   (226)

7.   An ancient saying, Atula,
not only said today:
They are blamed who silent sit,
who often speak they too are blamed,
they blame them saying little too, –
there's none in the world unblamed.   (227)

8.   There never was, there'll never be,
nor now is ever found
a person blamed exclusively
or one who's only praised.   (228)

9.   But those who are intelligent
praise one of flawless conduct, wise
in wisdom and virtue well-composed,
having observed him day by day.   (229)

10.   Who can blame that worthy one
like ornament of finest gold?
Even the devas praise him
by Brahma too he's praised.   (230)

11.   Physical roughness guard against,
have bodily self-restraint,
misconduct of body abandoning
good conduct cultivate.   (231)

12. Verbal roughness guard against,
    have verbal self-restraint
    misconduct of speech abandoning
    good conduct cultivate.   (232)

13. Mental roughness guard against,
    have mental self-restraint,
    misconduct of mind abandoning
    good conduct cultivate.   (233)

14. Restrained in body are the wise,
    in speech as well they are restrained,
    likewise are they restrained in mind,
    they're perfectly restrained.   (234)

NOTES

4.   **These conditions three** – the practice of truth-speaking, loving-kindness and generosity will be the appropriate karma for most people to gain rebirth among the gods of the sensual realm heavens.

5.   **Everlasting State** – Nirvana, so called because once attained it is not possible to fall away from that experience. This verse is one of the few that has remained unaltered in translation since the first of my efforts in 1966.

7.   **Atula** – the name of a layman who blamed various bhikkhus in these ways.

XVIII
MALAVAGGA
VERSES ON BLEMISHES

1. Now a withered leaf you are,
   and now Death's men draw near,
   now you stand at the parting place –
   but waybread have you none.   (235)

2. Make an island of yourself,
   quickly strive and wise become;
   spotless, cleansed of blemishes,
   go to the Nobles' subtle plane.   (236)

3. Even now the end draws near
   now you're off to the presence of death,
   along the way there is no rest –
   and waybread have you none.   (237)

4. Make an island of yourself,
   quickly strive and wise become;
   spotless, cleansed of blemishes,
   you'll not return, be born and decay.   (238)

5. Little by little, time after time,
   successively then let the sage
   blow away all blemishes
   just as smith with silver.   (239)

6. As rust arisen out of iron
   itself that iron eats away,
   so karmas done beyond what's wise
   lead to a woeful state. (240)

7. For oral tradition – non-recitation,
   in household life – non-exertion,
   the fair of form – when slovenly,
   a watchman's sloth: all blemishes. (241)

8. In woman, conduct culpable,
   with givers, avariciousness,
   all blemishes these evil things
   in this world or the next. (242)

9. More basic than these blemishes –
   is ignorance, worst of all.
   Abandoning this blemish then,
   be free of blemish monks! (243)

10. Easy the life for a shameless one
    who bold and froward as a crow,
    is slanderer and braggart too:
    this life's completely stained. (244)

11. But hard the life of a modest one
    who always seeks for purity.
    cheerful but not arrogant,
    pure of life, reflective. (245)

12. In the world who life destroys
    who utters words that are untrue,

who takes what is not freely given
or to another's partner goes.   (246)

13.   Or has distilled, fermented drinks,
      whoever is addicted thus
      extirpates the roots of self
      even here in this very world.   (247)

14.   Therefore friend remember this:
      hard to restrain are evil acts
      don't let greed and wickedness
      down drag you long in dukkha.   (248)

15.   People give as they have faith,
      as they are bright with joyfulness.
      Who's troubled over gifts received
      the food and drink that others get,
      neither in daytime nor by night
      will come to a collected mind.   (249)

16.   But who has severed envy's mind
      uprooted it, destroyed entire,
      indeed in daytime and by night
      will come to a collected mind.   (250)

17.   No fire's so hot as lust,
      no captor strong as anger,
      unequalled is delusion's net,
      no river broad as craving,   (251)

18.   Others' faults are easy to see
      yet hard to see are one's own,
      and so one winnows just like chaff

the faults of other people, while
hiding away those of one's own,
as crafty cheat the losing throw. (252)

19. Whoso sees others' faults,
taking offence, censorious,
pollutions spread for such a one
who's far from their exhaustion. (253)

20. In space there is no path,
no monk is there outside,
folk delight in manifoldness,
Tathagatas are manifold-free. (254)

21. In space there is no path,
no monk is there outside,
no thing conditioned ever lasts,
no Buddha's ever shaken. (255)

NOTES

1. **Waybread** – 'food for the journey', the provisions needed along the path of the dead being merits or good karmas.

2. **Nobles' subtle plane** – the Pure Abodes of the non-returners.

7. **Oral tradition** – there were no written books in the Buddha's day, though writing was used for commerce, etc. Religious 'texts' were carefully learnt by heart from teacher to pupil. 'Oral tradition' is only an approximate translation of 'manta', the Pali form of mantra.

9. **Unknowing** – avijjā, of the Four Noble Truths, see note on verses 190–191.

12–13 **Life destroys** – the Five Precepts of Buddhist laity. Each is usually prefixed by the declaration: "I undertake the training-rule to refrain from …"

20–21 **No monk … outside** – there can be none who have realized the Paths and Fruits of a Noble One outside the Buddha's Teachings because in other teachings the Four Noble Truths – the essence of Wisdom (paññā) to be realized in one's heart – are not taught, or only incompletely. This is the Comy's interpretation. Other more liberal explanations are possible. One is that there is no monk outside oneself, that is no peaceful one except in one's own heart. Then again, it could be interpreted as an elliptical way of saying 'there is no monk (just by his) outside (marks)'. This would agree with such verses as 264, 266, 269, 307.

    20.   **Manifoldness** – see note on verse 195.

XIX
DHAMMATTHAVAGGA
VERSES ON WHAT ACCORDS WITH DHARMA

1. Whoever judges hastily
   does Dharma not uphold,
   a wise one should investigate
   truth and untruth both. (256)

2. Who others guides impartially;
   with evenness and Dharma
   Dharma's guardian is that sage
   and set in Dharma's called. (257)

3. Just because articulate
   one's not thereby wise,
   hateless, fearless and secure,
   a 'wise one' thus is called. (258)

4. Just because articulate
   one's not a 'Dharma-holder'
   but one who's heard a little
   and Dharma in the body sees,
   that one's a Dharma-holder –
   not heedless of the Dharma. (259)

5. A man is not a Elder
   though his head be grey

he's just fully ripe in years
'aged-in-vain' he's called. (260)

6. In whom is truth and Dharma too,
    harmlessness, restraint, control,
    one steadfast, blemishes expelled,
    an Elder's rightly called. (261)

7. Not by eloquence alone,
    or by a lovely countenance
    is a person beautiful
    if jealous, boastful, mean. (262)

8. But 'beautiful' is called that one
    in whom these are completely shed
    uprooted, utterly destroyed,
    a wise one purged of hate. (263)

9. By shaven head no monk if then
    deceitful and disordered,
    engrossed in greed and selfishness
    how shall he be a monk? (264)

10. All evils altogether he
    subdues both fine and gross;
    having subdued all evil he
    indeed is called a monk: (265)

11. Because one begs from others
    by that alone no monk.
    The whole of Dharma doing,
    on that account a monk. (266)

12. Who both good and evil deeds
     has gone beyond with holy life,
     having discerned the world he fares
     a 'bhikkhu' he is called.   (267)

13. By silence one is not a sage
     if confused and ignorant,
     but the wise man as with scales
     weighs and takes the best.   (268)

14. Shunning evils utterly
     one is a sage, by that a sage;
     whoever both worlds knows
     for that one's called a sage.   (269)

15. By harming living beings
     not thus is one a 'Noble' man,
     by lack of harm to all that live
     one's called a 'Noble One'.   (270)

16. Not by vows and rituals
     or again by learning much
     or by meditative calm
     or by life in solitude,   (271)

17. Should you O bhikkhu, be content:
     'I've touched the bliss of letting go
     not enjoyed by common folk' –
     while unattained to pollutions' end.   (272)

NOTES

4.   **Dharma-holder** – not one who 'holds' Dharma from what he has remembered, but one whose heart is full of Dharma from penetration to it.

13.   **Silence ... sage** – play on the words 'mona' and 'muni'; see, note on verse 49.

15.   **Noble** – (ariya) a fisherman named Ariya was addressed with this verse.

17.   **Be content** – getting false confidence.

17.   **I've touched ... letting go** – a bhikkhu should not rest content with attainments less than the exhaustion of the pollutions.

XX
MAGGAVAGGA
VERSES ON THE PATH

1. Of paths the eightfold is the best,
    of truths the statements four,
    the passionless of teachings best,
    of humankind the Seer.   (273)

2. This is the path, no other's there
    for purity of insight;
    enter then upon this path
    bemusing Mara utterly.   (274)

3. Entered, then upon this path
    you'll make an end of dukkha.
    Freed by Knowledge from suffering's stings
    the Path's proclaimed by me.   (275)

4. Tathagatas proclaim the path
    but you're the ones to strive.
    Contemplatives who tread the path
    are freed from Mara's bonds.   (276)

5. When with wisdom one discerns
    transience of conditioned things:
    tired, from pain one turns away:
    truly the path to purity.   (277)

6. When with wisdom one discerns
   the dukkha of conditioned things
   tired, from pain one turns away:
   truly the path to purity.   (278)

7. When with wisdom one discerns
   all knowables are not a self:
   tired, from pain one turns away:
   truly the path to purity.   (279)

8. Though time to strive, not striving,
   while young and strong, yet indolent,
   lazy-minded with sluggish thought –
   wisdom's way an idler does not find.   (280)

9. In speech ever watchful, with mind
              well-restrained
   never with the body do unwholesomeness,
   so should one purify these three
              karma-paths
   winning the way made known by
              the seers.   (281)

10. From endeavour wisdom springs,
    lacking effort wisdom wanes;
    having known this twofold path
    to either progress or decline,
    so should one exhort oneself
    that wisdom may increase.   (282)

11. The 'would' cut down but not a tree,
    since from the 'would' fear is born;

having cut 'would' and 'wouldedness',
O bhikkhus, be without a 'would'.   (283)

12.   As long, indeed, as 'wouldedness'
      of man to woman is not cut,
      so long in bondage is one's mind,
      as milch-calf to the mother cow.   (284)

13.   Cut off affection for oneself
      as hand a lily in the fall
      cultivate this path of peace –
      Nirvana, by the Well-gone taught.   (285)

14.   Here shall I spend the rains,
      here the winter, here the summer:
      thus speculates the fool –
      the danger he knows not.   (286)

15.   One who has a clinging mind
      and finds delight in babes and herds
      Death does seize and carry away,
      as great flood a sleeping village.   (287)

16.   No sons are there for shelter.
      nor father, nor related folk;
      for one by the Ender seized upon
      in kin no shelter finds.   (288)

17.   Having understood this fact,
      the wise, by virtue well restrained
      swiftly then should clear the path
      leading to Nirvana.   (289)

NOTES

1.   **Paths ... eightfold** – The Noble Eightfold Path of which the first two factors concern wisdom: Right view, right intention; the next three, moral conduct: Right speech, right action, right livelihood; the last three meditation: Right effort, right mindfulness, right collectedness. See *The Word of the Buddha*, B.P.S. See 191.

1.   **Seer** – lit., One with Vision: the Buddha is best among all two-footed beings since possessed of both subtle and wisdom eyes or vision.

4.   **Tathagatas** – this word was used by the Buddha when speaking of himself, meaning 'One who has arrived at Reality'. But He and other Buddhas only proclaim the path, they do not force anyone to practise, nor do they save them.

5-7.   **Transience ... Dukkha ... Not a self** – the three characteristics of all living beings. All three apply to conditioned things such as mind and body, but only the last one applies to both the conditioned and the Unconditioned (=Nirvana).

5-7.   **Tired / turns away** – can also be translated: 'is disgusted with'.

9.   **Karma-paths** – ways of making karma.

11-12.   **Would ... wouldedness** – an easy pun on the word 'vana' in Pali which means both 'forest' and 'passions', but which is only just possible in English (with acknowledgments to Ven. Nyānamoli Thera) by playing on the words 'wood' and 'would' (in the sense of desire). 'Wouldedness' is the growing together of the trees, etc. or the tangled nature of the passions. See 344.

13.   **Well-gone** – Sugata, meaning one whose coming and going is auspicious, and whose final 'going out' (Parinibbana) is unexcelled.

14.   **Danger** – of decay, disease, death etc.

XXI
PAKINNAKAVAGGA
VERSES ON THE MISCELLANEOUS

1. If one should see great happiness
    in giving up small happiness,
    one wise the lesser would renounce
    the greater full discerning.   (290)

2. Whoso for self wants happiness
    by causing others pain,
    entangled in anger's tangles
    from anger's never free.   (291)

3. What should be done is left undone
    and done is what should not be done:
    ever the pollutions grow
    of those ones proud and heedless.   (292)

4. But those who always practise well
    bodily mindfulness,
    do never what should not be done
    and ever do what should be done;
    for mindful ones, the full aware,
    pollutions fade away.   (293)

5. One's mother and father having slain
    and then two warrior kings,

a realm as well its treasurer,
one goes immune, a paragon. (294)

6. One's mother and father having slain
and then two learned kings,
as well the fifth, a tiger fierce,
one goes immune, a paragon. (295)

7. Always well-awake and watchful
are the pupils of Gotama
who constantly by day and night
are mindful of the Buddha (296)

8. Always well-awake and watchful
are the pupils of Gotama
who constantly by day and night
are mindful of the Dharma. (297)

9. Always well-awake and watchful
are the pupils of Gotama
who constantly by day and night
are mindful of the Sangha. (298)

10. Always well-awake and watchful
are the pupils of Gotama
who constantly by day and night
are mindful of the body. (299)

11. Always well-awake and watchful
are the pupils of Gotama
whose minds by day and night
in harmlessness delight. (300)

12.   Always well-awake and watchful
       are the pupils of Gotama
       whose minds by day and night
       in meditation delight.   (301)

13.   Hard's leaving home, hard to delight in it,
       hard's household life, and dukkha too,
       dukkha to dwell with those dissimilar
       and dukkha falls upon the wanderer:
       be therefore not a wanderer,
       not one on whom this dukkha falls.   (302)

14.   Who's full of faith and virtue,
       of substance, high repute,
       is honoured everywhere
       wherever that one lives.   (303)

15.   Afar the true are manifest
       like Himalayan range:
       yet even here the false aren't seen
       as arrows shot by night.   (304)

16.   Alone one sits, alone one lies,
       alone one walks unweariedly,
       in solitude one tames oneself
       so in the woods will one delight.   (305)

NOTES

2.   **Pain** – dukkha, in Pali.

5–6. **One's mother ... a paragon** – two 'shock' verses spoken by the Buddha to parties of visiting bhikkhus. The bhikkhus were so startled that they developed deep attainments when hearing them. The commentary explains the terms in these verses as follows:

Mother = craving; **father** = the conceit 'I am'; **two warrior kings** = the two views of eternalism and annihilationism; **a realm** = the 12 bases of the senses and their objects (eye-sight, ear-sound … mind-dharmas); **treasurer** = passionate delight (in the 12 bases); **a Paragon** (Brahmana) = an Arahant, the pollutions destroyed. I have translated 'brahmana' with the word 'paragon', see notes to last chapter.

These verses are tests of a Dhammapada translation. In some translations one can find 'Though he has slain his mother and father …' still he is pure since enlightened. This is erroneous. The un-enlightened can slay – and suffer the results. The Enlightened cannot purposely kill any creature. And the Pāli has no 'though' in it at all.

6. **Two learned kings** – the two opposed views mentioned above.

6. **The fifth a tiger** – the Commentary says the fifth of the five Hindrances (to deep meditation) which is uncertainty is compared to the danger of a tiger-infested path.

13. **Leaving home** – pabbajjā, going forth from home to homelessness.

13. **Wanderer** – one who wanders in the round of saṁsāra, from life to life.

XXII
NIRAYAVAGGA
VERSES ON HELL

1. With one denying truth there goes to hell
    that one who having done says 'I did not'.
    Humans having made some karmas base
    equal are they in the other world.   (306)

2. Many who wear the yellow robe
    are unrestrained in evil things,
    these evil ones by evil deeds
    in hell do they arise.   (307)

3. Better to eat a ball of iron
    glowing as flame of fire
    than one should eat the country's alms
    immoral and unrestrained.   (308)

4. Four things befall that heedless one
    sleeping with one who's wed:
    demerit gained but not good sleep,
    third is blame while fourth is hell.   (309)

5. Demerit's gained and evil birth,
    scared man and woman – brief their joy,
    the king decrees a heavy doom:
    so none should sleep with one who's wed. (310)

6.   As blady grass when wrongly grasped
      lacerates the hand,
      so mishandled monastic life
      drags one to hell.   (311)

7.   Whatever of karmas slack
      whatever of vows corrupt,
      a faltering in the holy life
      never brings ample fruit.   (312)

8.   If there's aught that should be done,
      let it be done then steadily
      in truth a slack monastic life
      all the more stirs up the dust.   (313)

9.   Better an evil deed not done –
      for misdeed later on torments.
      Better done is deed that's good
      which done, does not torment.   (314)

10.   Even as a border town
      guarded within and without,
      so should you protect yourselves.
      Do not let this moment pass,
      for when this moment's gone
            they grieve
      sending themselves to hell.   (315)

11.   They are ashamed where shame is not
      but where is shame are not ashamed,
      so embracing evil views
      such beings go to an evil birth.   (316)

12. They are afraid where fear is not
     but where is fear are unafraid
     so embracing evil views
     such beings go to an evil birth.   (317)

13. Faults they see where fault is not
     but where is fault they see it not
     so embracing evil views
     such beings go to an evil birth.   (318)

14. A fault they understand as such,
     they know as well where fault is not
     so embracing virtuous views
     beings go to a happy birth.   (319)

NOTES

1.   **Hell** – impermanent as all other states of birth, not everlasting. Finite evil karmas must give rise to finite evil states, not to infinite ones! The worst among all possible planes of birth with continuous sufferings.

2.   **The yellow robe** – the yellow robes of a samana or bhikkhu. See notes on verses 9–10.

10. **This moment** – this opportunity which is hard to get with a Buddha's arising,   the Dharma's teachings, health, right views, etc. Ultimately the only time when Dharma can be practised or realised.

10. **Sending** – one sends oneself to hell (by evil karma, especially that involving killing and cruelty), one is not sent by another. 'Themselves' is not in Pāli, where the sense is obvious without it.

11–14. **Views... evil views**: 'there is no such thing as karma', or 'actions have no results for oneself', or 'there is no other life than this'. Virtuous views affirm that we make karma, that it has results now and in future.

XXIII
NĀGAVAGGA
VERSES ON THE GREAT

1.   Many folk are ill-behaved
     but I shall endure abuse,
     as elephant on battlefield
     arrows shot from a bow.   (320)

2.   The tusker tamed they lead in crowds
     the king he mounts the tamed;
     best of humans are the tamed
     who can endure abuse.   (321)

3.   Excellent are mules when tamed
     and thoroughbreds from Sindh,
     noble the elephants of state,
     still better one self-tamed.   (322)

4.   Surely not on mounts like these
     one goes the Unfrequented Way,
     rather by oneself well-tamed
     as tusker tamed by taming goes.   (323)

5.   The tusker with the name Dhanapalaka
     pungent rut exuding, uncontrolled,
     when bound a mouthful doesn't eat –
     with longing he recalls his forest home. (324)

6. A sluggard stupid steeped in gluttony,
    engrossed in sleep, who wallows as he lies,
    like a great porker gorged with swill,
    comes ever and again into a womb.   (325)

7. Formerly this wandering mind, a wanderer,
    went where it wished, where whim,
            where pleasure led;
    wisely today will I restrain it,
    as trainer's hook, an elephant in rut.   (326)

8. Do you delight in heedfulness
    and guard your own minds well!
    Draw yourselves from evil ways
    as tusker stuck in mud.   (327)

9. If for practice one finds a friend,
    prudent, well-behaved and wise,
    mindful, joyful, live with him
    all troubles overcoming.   (328)

10. If for practice one finds no friend,
    prudent, well-behaved and wise,
    as king be leaving conquered land,
    fare alone as elephant in the wilds.   (329)

11. Better it is to live alone
    for with a fool's no fellowship
    no evils do, be free of care
    fare alone as elephant in the wilds.   (330)

12. Blest are friends when one's in need
    blest contentment with whatever is

blessed is merit when life is at an end,
abandoning all dukkha – blessedness.   (331)

13.   Happiness, serving mother here,
serving one's father – happiness,
happiness serving the peaceful here,
Pure Ones to serve is happiness.   (332)

14.   Blest is virtue till life's end
and blest a faith that's standing firm,
blest is one who wisdom gains
and blest the non-doing of evil.   (333)

NOTES

1.   **Elephant** – nāga, this word also refers to the serpent-spirits and to great human beings, such as a Buddha. In this chapter it has the first and third meanings, hence the translation of the title.

2.   **Tamed** – danta, there is a pun here which English cannot reproduce: danta, past part, of verb 'to tame', and danta, a tooth or tusk (see dental, dentist, etc.). An elephant is 'one with tusks' or 'a tamed one'.

5.   **Dhanapalaka** – an elephant which although held in luxurious captivity by a king yearned to return to the forest where it cared for its old, blind mother.

9–10. **Friend** – a Noble friend (kalyānamitra), one who teaches Dharma from his own experience.

XXIV
TANHĀVAGGA
VERSES ON CRAVING

1. As creeping ivy craving grows
    in one living carelessly.
    Like this, one leaps from life to life
    as ape in the forest seeking fruit.   (334)

2. Who in this world is overcome
    by contemptible craving poison-filled,
    for such a one do sorrows grow
    as meadow-grass well rained upon.   (335)

3. Who in this world does overcome
    contemptible craving hard to cross,
    for such a one do sorrows fall
    like water drops from a lotus leaf.   (336)

4. Prosperity to you, I say,
    to all assembled here!
    As one looks for fragrant roots
    so craving extirpate.
    Let Mara break you not again,
    again as torrent a reed!   (337)

5. As a tree though felled shoots up again
    while roots are safe and firm

so this dukkha grows again,
while latent craving's not removed.　　(338)

6.　For whom the six and thirty streams
　　flow oft to the delightful,
　　floods of thoughts sprung from lust
　　flood that one of evil view.　　(339)

7.　Everywhere these streams are swirling,
　　craving's creeper grows and climbs;
　　seeing the craving-creeper there
　　with wisdom cut its root!　　(340)

8.　Happy-minded humans are
　　attached to streaming senses
　　settled in comfort, seeking joy
　　such people come to birth and decay.　　(341)

9.　Who follow craving are assailed,
　　they tremble as the hare ensnared
　　bonds and fetters bind them fast,
　　again, again they come to pain.　　(342)

10.　Who follow craving are assailed,
　　they tremble as the hare ensnared,
　　so therefore should they craving quell
　　whose aim is passionlessness.　　(343)

11.　Who without 'wouldness' inclines to
　　　　the wood,
　　in the wood free to 'wouldness' he returns.
　　Come regard this person
　　who free returns to fetters!　　(344)

12. The bonds of iron or wood or hemp
    are not so strong – so say the wise,
    but beings attached with longing
            and lust
    to children, wives, jewelled ornaments – (345)

13. This bond is strong, proclaim the wise
    down-dragging, pliable, hard to loose:
    this having severed, home do they leave
    not longing for pleasures of senses.   (346)

14. Ensnared in passion back they fall
    as spider on a self-spun web,
    this having severed, wander the wise
    longingless, all pain renounced.   (347)

15. The past let go, the future too,
    let go to the present: be beyond becoming –
    with mind released in every way
    you'll come no more to birth-decay.   (348)

16. One who beauty contemplates
    with agitated thoughts and active lust,
    for that one craving grows the more
    then strengthens all the bonds.   (349)

17. But who delights in calming thoughts
    develops foulness mindfully,
    that one indeed will make an end,
    will sever Mara's bonds.   (350)

18. One who's fearless, reached the End,
    free of craving, blemish free,

who has becoming's thorn plucked out –
last his bodily congeries.   (351)

19.   One of clinging-craving free
who's skilled in ways of chanting,
knowing the wording sequence,
of what precedes and follows
who has a final body,
one greatly wise, Great Person's called. (352)

20.   Beyond all being, knowing all,
unsoiled by dharmas all am I,
left all and freed by craving's end,
by self I've known, whom Teacher call? (353)

21.   Gift of the Dharma surpasses all gifts
taste of the Dharma betters all tastes,
delight in the Dharma bests other
        delights,
one craving-exhausted conquers all ill. (354)

22.   Riches ruin a foolish one
but not one questing the Beyond;
craving for wealth the foolish one
ruins himself as though it were others. (355)

23.   Weeds, a failing of fields,
lust's a human failing,
thus offerings to the lustless
bear abundant fruit.   (356)

24.   Weeds, a failing of fields,
hate's a human failing,

hence offerings to the hateless
bear abundant fruit. (357)

25. Weeds, a failing of fields,
delusion – human failing,
so gifts to the undeluded
bear abundant fruit. (358)

26. Weeds, a failing of fields,
desire's a human failing,
so gifts to the desireless
bear abundant fruit. (359)

NOTES

1. **Ivy** – see note on verse 162.
6. **Six and thirty streams** – of craving, which is of three kinds: for sense-pleasures, for existence, for non-existence; these being multiplied by the 12 bases (six internal, six external), to make 36 'streams'.
11. **Wouldness** – see note on verses 283–284.
15. **Let go ...** – spoken to an acrobat poised on the top of a bamboo pole! See note on verse 421.
16–17. See note on verses 7–8. Foulness, lit., unattractiveness.
18. **Reached the End** – attained to Nirvana.
20. **Whom Teacher call?** – this verse was spoken to a naked ascetic outside Benares, before the Buddha taught the five recluses with the First Sermon.
21. **Ill** – dukkha.
23–26. **Weeds** – lit. a strong piercing kind of grass.

XXXV
BHIKKHUVAGGA
VERSES ON THE MONK

1. Right is restraint in eye,
   restraint in ear is right,
   right is restraint in nose,
   restraint in tongue is right. (360)

2. Right is restraint in body,
   restraint in speech is right,
   right is restraint in mind,
   everywhere restraint is right;
   a monk who's everywhere restrained
   is from all dukkha free. (361)

3. Controlled in hands, controlled in feet,
   in speech controlled, supremely well
            controlled,
   delighting in inward collectedness,
   alone, content they call him 'monk'. (362)

4. That monk who is controlled in tongue,
   with wisdom speaks and is not proud,
   who theory and practice can expound
   sweet as honey is his speech. (363)

5.   The monk who in the Dharma dwells,
in Dharma delighting and pondering
remembering the Dharma – he
does not decline from Dharma True.   (364)

6.   He should not disdain his gains
nor live of others envious,
the monk of others envious
does not attain collectedness.   (365)

7.   Though little he receive
disdaining not his gains
pure of life and keen,
that monk do gods all praise   (366)

8.   For whom there is no making 'mine'
towards all name and form,
who does not grieve for what is not,
a monk is truly called.   (367)

9.   A monk who dwells in kindly love,
bright in the Buddha's Teaching,
can come to the Place of Peace –
bliss of calming the conditioned.   (368)

10.   Bail out this boat, O monk,
when emptied it will swiftly move
having severed lust and hate
thus to Nibbāna go.   (369)

11.   Five cut off and five forsake,
a further five then cultivate,

a monk who's from five fetters free
is called a 'Forder-of-the-flood'. (370)

12. Meditate monks and don't be heedless!
Don't let pleasures whirl the mind!
Heedless, gulp not down a glob of iron,
then when burning do not wail
'It is dukkha'. (371)

13. No concentration wisdom lacks
no wisdom concentration lacks;
in whom are both these qualities
is in Nibbana's presence. (372)

14. The bhikkhu gone to a lonely place
who is of peaceful heart,
in-sees Dharma rightly,
knows superhuman joy. (373)

15. Whenever one reflects
on aggregates' arise and fall,
one rapture gains and joy,
for the gnostic, Deathlessness. (374)

16. Here's indeed the starting point
for that monk with wisdom:
sense-control, contentment too,
restraint to limit 'freedom's' ways
and company of noble friends
who're pure of livelihood and keen. (375)

17. One should be hospitable
and skilled in good behaviour,

thereby greatly joyful
come to dukkha's end. (376)

18. Just as the jasmine sheds
its shrivelled flowers all,
O bhikkhus, so should you
lust, aversion shed. (377)

19. Of peaceful body, peaceful speech,
peaceful, well-composed of heart,
having spewed out of the world's
        desires –
'truly peaceful' that monk is called. (378)

20. By yourself exhort yourself!
By yourself restrain yourself!
Thus mindful and self-guarded too
happily you will live. (379)

21. Oneself is refuge of oneself
and one is pathway for oneself:
therefore one should check oneself
as merchant does a splendid horse. (380)

22. The monk who's full of joy and faith
bright in the Buddha's Teaching
will reach the Place of Peace –
bliss of calming the conditioned. (381)

23. Surely that youthful monk
who strives in the Buddha's Teaching
illumines all this world
as moon when freed from clouds. (382)

NOTES

8. **Name and form** – name (nāma) means mind, the 'namer' of everything; form is a term for material things, including body.

10. **Boat** – the body, the water to be emptied out being unwholesome thoughts.

11. **Five ...** – cut off the five fetters (samyojana) binding to the realm of sensual desires, give up the five fetters which bind to the realms of subtle form and of formlessness (for these see note on verse. 31); cultivate, the five faculties (indriya) – confidence, effort, mindfulness, collectedness and wisdom; 'from five fetters free', (fetters here – sanga) – lust, aversion, delusion, conceit and wrong view.

14. **In-sees** – sees with insight (vipassanā) that his own mind-body continuity are impermanent, dukkha and non-self. See verse 174.

15. **Aggregates** – khanda, the five which are a complete analysis of all beings in the realm of sensual desire: body, feeling, recognition, volitions, consciousness.

16. **'Freedom's' ways** – see note on verse 185.

17. **Hospitable** – doing the duties of a host towards a guest.

19. See verse 96.

21. **Pathway** – one is pathway for oneself because the karma which one makes in the present will fruit some time in the future and become the path along which one goes.

XXVI
BRAHMAṆAVAGGA
VERSES ON THE BRAHMIN

1. O brahmin strive and cleave the stream
   desires of sense discard,
   knowing conditioned things' decay
   be Knower-of-the-Uncreate. (383)

2. When by the twofold Dharma
   a Brahmin's gone beyond
   all the bonds of One-who-Knows
   have wholly disappeared. (384)

3. For whom is found no near or far,
   and neither near-and-far,
   free of fear and fetter free:
   One such I say's a paragon. (385)

4. Seated stainless, concentrated,
   who's work is done, who's free of taint,
   having attained the highest aim:
   One such I say's a paragon. (386)

5. The sun is bright by day,
   the moon enlightens night,
   armoured shines the warrior,
   contemplative the Brahmana:

but all the day and night-time too
resplendent does the Buddha shine.   (387)

6. By 'barring-out-badness' brahmin
        one's called
    and one is a monk by conduct serene,
    'banishing blemishes' out of oneself
    hence one is known as 'one who
        left home'.   (388)

7. One should not strike a Brahmin,
    nor for that would he react.
    Shame! who beats a Brahmin,
    more shame if he react!   (389)

8. For the Brahmin no small benefit
    when mind's aloof from what is dear.
    As much he turns away from harm
    so much indeed does dukkha die.   (390)

9. In whom is no wrong-doing
    by body, speech or mind,
    in these three ways restrained:
    One such I say's a paragon.   (391)

10. Devoutly that one honour,
    as a brahmin sacred fire,
    from whom one knows the Dharma
    by the Perfect Buddha taught.   (392)

11. Not by birth a brahmin
    not coiled up hair, not family:

in whom are truth and Dharma too
pure is he, a Brahmin's he.   (393)

12. Dimwit! What's the coiled hair for?
     For what your deerskin cloak?
     Within you are acquisitive,
     you decorate without!   (394)

13. One enduring rag-robes, lean,
     with body overspread by veins,
     lone in the woods who meditates:
     One such I say's a paragon.   (395)

14. Him I call not brahmin though
     born from brahmin mother's line –
     for if with sense of ownership
     he's just supercilious;
     but owning nothing and unattached,
     one such I say's a paragon.   (396)

15. Who fetters all has severed,
     Who trembles not at all,
     gone beyond ties, free from bonds:
     One such I say's a paragon.   (397)

16. Having cut the strap and reins,
     the rope and bridle too,
     and tipped the shafts: as One Awake
     One such I say's a paragon.   (398)

17. Who angerless endures abuse,
     beating and imprisonment,

with patience-power, an armed might:
One such I say's a paragon. (399)

18. Who's angerless and dutiful,
of virtue full and free of lust,
who's tamed, to final body come:
One such I say's a paragon. (400)

19. Like water drop on lotus leaf,
or mustard seed on needle point,
whoso clings not to sensual things:
One such I say's a paragon. (401)

20. Here who comes to know
exhaustion of all dukkha,
laid down the burden, free from bonds:
One such I say's a paragon. (402)

21. Skilled in the Path, what's not-the-Path,
in wisdom deep, sagacious one,
having attained the highest aim:
One such I say's a paragon. (403)

22. Not intimate with those gone forth
nor with those who dwell at home,
without a shelter, wishes few:
One such I say's a paragon. (404)

23. Who has renounced all force
to beings weak and strong,
who causes not to kill nor kills:
One such I say's a paragon. (405)

24. Among the hostile, friendly,
     among the violent, cool,
     detached amidst the passionate:
     One such I say's a paragon.   (406)

25. From whoever lust and hate
     conceit, contempt have dropped away
     as mustard seed from needle point:
     One such I say's a paragon.   (407)

26. Who utters speech instructive,
     true and gentle too,
     who gives offence to none:
     One such I say's a paragon.   (408)

27. Who in the world will never take
     what is not given – long or short,
     the great or small, the fair or foul:
     One such I say's a paragon.   (409)

28. In whom there are no longings found
     in this world or the next,
     longingless and free from bonds:
     One such I say's a paragon.   (410)

29. In whom is no dependence found,
     with Final Knowledge, freed from doubt,
     duly won to the Deathless depths:
     One such I say's a paragon.   (411)

30. Here who's gone beyond both bonds
     to goodness and to evil too,

who is sorrowless, stainless, pure:
One such I say's a paragon. (412)

31. Vanished all love of being,
like the moon, unblemished, pure,
him, serene and undisturbed:
One such I say's a paragon. (413)

32. Who's overpassed this difficult path,
delusion's bond, the wandering-on,
who's crossed beyond, contemplative,
craving not, no questions left,
no clinging's fuel so cool become:
One such I say's a paragon. (414)

33. Who has abandoned lusting here,
as homeless one renouncing all,
lust and becoming all consumed:
One such I say's a paragon. (415)

34. Who has abandoned craving here,
as homeless one renouncing all,
craving, becoming, all consumed:
One such I say's a paragon. (416)

35. Abandoned all the human bonds
and gone beyond the bonds of gods,
unbound one is from every bond:
One such I say's a paragon. (417)

36. Abandoned boredom and delight,
become quite cool and assetless,

a Hero, All Worlds Conqueror:
One such I say's a paragon   (418)

37.   Whoever knows of beings' death,
their being born in every way,
unshackled, faring well, Awake:
One such I say's a paragon.   (419)

38.   Whose destination is unknown
to humans, spirits or to gods,
pollutions faded, Arahat:
One such I say's a paragon   (420)

39.   For whom there is no ownership
before or after or midway,
owning nothing and unattached:
One such I say's a paragon.   (421)

40.   One noble, most excellent, heroic too,
the great sage and one who conquers all,
who's faultless, washen, one Awake:
One such I say's a paragon.   (422)

41.   Who knows his former births
and sees the states of bliss and woe
and then who wins the waste of births,
a sage supreme with wisdom won,
complete in all accomplishments:
One such I say's a paragon.   (423)

NOTES

1. **Brahmin** – the traditional Indian caste meaning – a brahmin priest, or born of brahmin parents. See note on 3 below. I have occasionally left the Pali word brahmana.

1. **Uncreate** – see note on verse 97.

2. **Twofold dharma** – of calm (samatha) and vipassana (insight); two aspects of meditation necessary for Enlightenment. See 372.

3. **Near or far ...** – 'near' = six internal sense bases (eye... mind), 'far' = six external object bases (sight-object, etc.), **'near-and-far'** = not grasping anything as me and mine. This implies a non-dual view.

3. **One such I say's a paragon** – lit. 'that one I call a brahmin'. The Buddha here uses the word 'brahmin' not to mean a member of the brahmin caste, nor a Hindu priest, but in the sense given it in several places in Pali, 'one who is pure or excellent', hence my translation. The disadvantage of this translation is that the connection is lost when this term is not translated.

6. **'Barring-out-badness'...** – punning definitions by the Buddha of three important terms.

12. **Coiled hair...** – such were marks of the brahminical and other non-Buddhist ascetics, which were sometimes, as here, just for outward show.

14. **Supercilious** – one who uses a familiar form of address suited to a junior or inferior when addressing a religious teacher or other respected person. (The former use of 'thou' in English). Brahmins, who considered themselves superior to all by birth were often supercilious and even addressed the Buddha familiarly, "Bho Gotama ..."

16. **Strap...** = aversion, **reins** = craving, **rope** = wrong views, **bridle** = proclivities to defilement, **shafts** = unknowing (of Four Noble Truths), **as one Awake** = Buddha.

23. **Renounced all force** – lit. laid down the stick, put aside violence.

24. **Cool** – nibbuta, become completely cool since the fires of greed, aversion and delusion have gone out for want of the fuel of grasping; attained to Nirvana.

29. **Duly won** – by gradual development of the mind (through moral conduct or precepts, meditation and wisdom) attained to Deathlessness, to Nirvana.

32. **Wandering on** – saṁsāra, see 95.

36. **Assetless** – without upadhi, of four sorts: the five groups (khandha, seen n. on 39 below), the defilements (kilesa), karma-making thoughts (abhisankhāra), and sense desires (kāma).

38.   **Destination** – gati, place of birth due to past karma. But a Buddha has exhausted past karma and makes no more, so his destination is not 'known', is not explicable in words. A Buddha after death of the body does not exist, nor not exist, nor both exist and not exist, nor neither exist nor not exist – whatever this means!

39.   **Before...** – to ownership or attachment to past, future or present groups (body, feeling, recognition, volitions, consciousness). See 348, 396.

40.   **Washen** – a brahminical term which for them implied ritual bathing (three times a day and sometimes in very cold water) which as an ascetic practice or penance was supposed to wash away one's sins. The Buddha points out that water, a physical element, however 'holy' it is said to be, can never wash away evil karma, which is not physical but of the mind. One has to wash away the defilements (greed, etc.) with the cleansing power of wisdom.

41.   **A sage ... accomplishments** – reached to the topmost height by comprehending what should be comprehended (i.e. dukkha); abandoning what should be abandoned (the causal arising of dukkha); realising what should be realized (the cessation of dukkha); developing what should be developed (the Noble Eightfold Path leading to the cessation of dukkha).